Portrait of the Artist
As a Young Superman

1876, aged 20.

Shaw in his Jaeger Suit. Circa 1885.

Portrait of the Artist
As a Young Superman

A Study of Shaw's Novels

R. F. Dietrich

No person is real until he has been transmuted
into a work of art.

BERNARD SHAW

University of Florida Press
Gainesville / 1969

A University of Florida Press Book

Library of Congress
Catalog Card No. 75–77613
SBN 8130–0277–X

PRINTED FOR THE PUBLISHER BY
VAUGHAN PRINTERS, INCORPORATED
ORLANDO, FLORIDA

Dedicated to

Norbert F. O'Donnell
In Memoriam

and to

J. Russell Reaver

Preface

In writing about the novels of Bernard Shaw, the critic encounters special problems, problems created largely by Shaw's being renowned as a dramatist rather than a novelist. Shaw's five novels were completed nearly a decade before his first play was produced, and because of this considerable gap in time the curious assumption has grown that Shaw sprang spontaneously into greatness as a dramatist at the rather advanced age of thirty-six, much as the people in his *Back to Methuselah* emerge fully grown from eggs. The truth is that as with all great writers there was long preparation for this emergence, and the novels tell the very interesting story of this preparation.

Were one writing on a central theme in the novels of Thomas Hardy or Charles Dickens, one could go right to the point, for readers could be expected to be familiar with most of the plots, and as the reputations of Hardy and Dickens are fairly well established, very little would need to be done in the way of justifying their art. Such is not the case with the novels of Bernard Shaw. Shaw's reputation as a major dramatist (not to mention his fame as a critic, raconteur, orator, gadfly, and all-round public figure) has served to obscure the novels to the point where they are seldom read and even more seldom criticized. Critics have often pretended that the novels either do not exist, or should never have been written. For one thing, there is so much of Shaw to read that the average critic never gets further than the major plays and prefaces, and even the Shavian enthusiast is skip-reading by the time he reaches the novels. For another thing, the novels are generally not as good as the best of the plays, and since scholarship is long, life short, the critic can argue that he has better things to do than ponder Shaw's novels.

The novels do not deserve such obscurity, but the psychology of the critic makes it almost inevitable. No critic, especially nowadays, likes to be accused of hero-worship. Being a Balanced Critic means to scorn the bad as well as praise the good in one's particular literary hero. The trouble with Shaw as a subject for criticism is that he does not lend himself to balanced criticism. Rather he inspires a religious fervor on the part of his disciples that, in the heat of argument, seems like fanaticism. I can remember one American Lit. man shaking his head at the spectacle of three Shavians excitedly defending "their boy" against any and all attacks. How, said the American Lit. man, can responsible criticism come from this? A good question, and one that many Shavians have undoubtedly asked themselves from the very first devout article ever published on Shaw.

The solution to the problem has not been a very happy one. When the critics have not ignored the novels altogether, in their frantic search for something to deplore they have too frequently achieved the illusion of being Balanced Critics by beating the novels to death. In piling ridicules upon the novels, the critics cleverly escape the charge of Shaviolatry. Furthermore, they do so without much disturbing their consciences, for has not Shaw himself offered up the novels for just such a sacrifice? One can find plenty of disclaimers of the novels among Shaw's own writings (as, for instance, he once confessed of his novels, "I am ashamed of the whole boodle of them"[1]). If the critic doesn't pay much attention to the context of Shaw's expressed opinions on his novels, he can make a very good case for those opinions being low indeed.

But such violence upon the novels is hardly fair, for there are quite as many indications that Shaw thought highly of his early works and wished them well. As Archibald Henderson infers, Shaw "publicly pretended to hate his novels, but in private he entertained for them a sneaking sort of affection."[2] Stanley

1. Bernard Shaw, *Collected Letters 1874–1897*, ed. Dan H. Laurence, p. 179. For publishing information concerning the cited works, see the Bibliography.

2. Archibald Henderson, *George Bernard Shaw: Man of the Century*, p. 120.

Weintraub further notices that "although he publicly deni-
grated the nearly stillborn novels of his nonage, he carefully
preserved the mice-chewed manuscripts for decades, and be-
laboured publishers about them even after he had loudly declared them dead."[3] The more Shaw protested the worthlessness
of his youthful efforts, the more he seemed to secretly value
those efforts. "My works are magnificent," he once confided to
a publisher, "but they are not business."[4]

The task of arranging the present book is thus complicated
to the possible detriment of the book's unity. For a perfectly
unified and tightly reasoned argument, one probably ought to
concentrate on the significance of the novels and reserve other
considerations such as the art of the novels for other books.
Certainly the argument would be easier to control if that plan
were followed. Unfortunately, as I cannot count on either my
readers having read the novels (or remembering the plots if
they have read them), or their having reached a sufficient appreciation of the novels' art, I find myself called upon to provide efficient plot summaries and to prove that the novels are
intrinsically valuable as objects of art. Undoubtedly a reader
is likely to attend to my thesis much more closely if he has first
been convinced of the intrinsic worth of the novels. For that
reason, I have placed a substantial essay on the art of the novels
early in this book before I explicitly launch my main argument.
In discussing Shaw's art, however, I have gotten over the difficulty of maintaining unity by discussing that art in a way that
sets up what I have to say later about the significance of the
novels. The point that I am driving at throughout, and the
point that the section on Shaw's art implicitly prepares for, is
that a great deal of the significance of the novels lies in their
art, in that Shaw used the art of the novel to pursue the greater
art of personality.

Perhaps I can best define my main argument by making clear
what it is not. I have not written a book showing how impor-

3. Stanley Weintraub, introduction to Shaw, *An Unfinished Novel*,
p. 4.

4. *Collected Letters 1874–1897*, p. 178.

tant Shaw's novels are as a reservoir of characters and situations for the future dramatist. Stanley Weintraub has already
done this, for one thing, and, for another, I wish to escape the
habitual assumption of too much Shaw criticism that the novels
are not valuable in themselves. Equally peripheral to my study
is a consideration of the novels as guides to the merely external
life of their author. Both Weintraub and John von Behren
Rodenbeck have substantial material of this sort in disserta-
tions. Nor am I concerned here with textual matters, except in
a few cases in which Shaw's revisions have some bearing upon
my thesis. The work on textual analysis done by both Weintraub and Rodenbeck promises more detailed considerations in
the future of Shaw as editor. As Robert Hogan, Weintraub,
and Rodenbeck have all written insightfully on how Shaw's
novels place in the context of their period, I see no reason to
expand on why and how Shaw's novels are like or unlike those
of Hardy, Dickens, James, etc. In all this, my aim is to avoid
the notion that Shaw's novels are valuable only insofar as they
shed light on some other area. What I want to do is shed light
on the novels themselves. My concentration therefore is to be
not on the novels as embryo plays, not on the novels as period
pieces, not on the novels as external autobiography, and not on
the novels as problems for textual analysis, but rather on the
novels themselves as they reveal the motive for and the method
of their creation, i.e., as they reveal the artful shaping of that
very extraordinary human being, the young Bernard Shaw of
1879–83. The novels show that Shaw was a considerable artist
and personality long before he achieved any sort of fame as a
dramatist or public figure.

In quoting from Shaw's novels, I follow the Shavian conventions of spelling and punctuation. The reader should not be
alarmed upon discovering omitted apostrophes or unusual spell-
ings, for they are simply manifestations of Shaw's Morrisian
concern for the book beautiful.

Finally, I wish to thank the University of Delaware for
granting me a Summer Faculty Fellowship in order that I might
finish this project of several years duration.

Contents

Portrait of the Artist
As a Young Superman

A Study of Shaw's Novels

An Introduction to the Novels

I never had anything accepted; but if I had never written the five long novels and the bushel of articles that were refused, I should not have been able to do the work that finally offered itself to me. . . . You must keep on knocking your head against the stone wall until it gives way. Only, remember the saying, "Knock, and it shall be opened unto you." There's no use in waiting if you don't knock.

BERNARD SHAW
Letter to Florence Farr

I have a great respect for the priggish conscientiousness of my first efforts. They prove too that, like Goethe, I knew all along, and have added more to my power of handling, illustrating, and addressing my material than to the material itself.

BERNARD SHAW
Preface to *Immaturity*

As to the literary execution of the books, I suppose it will not now be questioned that I am no mere man of genius, but a conscientious workman as well.

"Mr. Bernard Shaw's Works of Fiction
Reviewed by Himself"

The History of the Novels

A study of Bernard Shaw's five novels at this time would be incomplete without some account of the manner in which the novels came into being. This story is most completely told in Henderson's biographies and Weintraub's introduction to *An Unfinished Novel*. A briefer version is in order here.

The story begins with Shaw's exodus from Dublin in 1876. Leaving behind a recently deceased sister, a somewhat broken, impecunious father, and a terribly unfulfilling job as a clerk in a prominent firm of Dublin realtors, he went to London to live with his mother, who had separated from the family shortly before to support herself by teaching voice. Rather generously she supported her son as well, at an age when most mothers would ask their sons to support them. This willingness to be the bread-winner left her son with an opportunity to educate himself in life and art.

Jobs were hard to come by in London for an immigrant Irish-man of "shabby gentility," and Shaw compounded the difficulty by instinctively avoiding the few opportunities that came his way. Later he joked about his horror of earning his living by honest labor. Thus for years Shaw was unemployed except for a short stretch as a clerk for a telephone company in 1879 and a few assignments as literary ghost for his mother's music part-ner, George Vandaleur Lee. Finally, at the insistence of William Archer, Shaw was hired in 1885–86 as an art and music critic and book reviewer for such various publications as the *Dramatic Review,* the *Magazine of Music,* the *Pall Mall Gazette,* and the *World.* Those years of chronic unemployment must have been demoralizing for Shaw were they not redeemed by the young man's habit of keeping himself busy. "My office training had left me with a habit of doing something regularly every day as a fundamental condition of industry as distinguished from idleness."[1]

1. Bernard Shaw, *Immaturity*, p. xxxvii.

Certainly the leisure afforded by his mother's generosity was not idly wasted. Many hours were spent in the Reading Room of the British Museum acquiring a comprehensive if unsystematic education. The world of intellect was his natural home, and he later claimed that he was at home "only with the mighty dead."[2] Of greatest relevance was his wide reading in the English novel, the Victorian success of which as the dominant genre in literature undoubtedly made the novel seem the obvious form for the young tyro seeking literary fame. Victorian drama being the corpse it was, Shaw was typical of the young writer of that day in his almost automatic choice of the novel as his form.

So he began writing novels, with a persistence indeed like Anthony Trollope's. For five years Shaw religiously wrote five pages a day, inspired or not. This argues an unusual industry, but even more astounding is the way he learned to write without hope or despair, for his novels were seemingly unpublishable. He spent an increasing amount of time and money sending his novels to every publisher he knew. But the little brown packages kept returning, sometimes with encouraging if somewhat confusing letters from the baffled readers, always without remuneration.

The novels did not experience publication until in 1884 Henry Hyde Champion serialized the last novel, *An Unsocial Socialist,* in his little socialist magazine, *To-Day,* between March and December. Then in 1887 the novel was put out under one cover in a cheap edition by Swann Sonnenschein & Co. The 1884 serialization paid Shaw nothing, but it did get him started. Thereafter the other novels, with one exception, were published in the inverse order of their creation. *Cashel Byron's Profession,* novel number four, was serialized second in *To-Day* between April 1885 and March 1886. Its relative popularity caused a book edition to be published soon after. In Annie Besant's *Our Corner* appeared *The Irrational Knot* from April 1885 to February 1887 and *Love Among the Artists* from November 1887 to December 1888, novels number two and three. Only *Immaturity,* first to be created and last to be pub-

2. *Ibid.,* p. xliii.

lished, avoided serialization, being brought out in a book edition in 1930 as part of the author's *Standard Edition*. Not long after Shaw achieved fame as a dramatist the other novels were printed in book editions.

Shaw insists that in revising the novels for publication he made very few changes, humanizing a passage here and daubing in a bit of socialism there. In fact, however, he made considerable revisions in at least one of his novels, *The Irrational Knot*, cutting out two whole chapters from the *Our Corner* version. In the other novels the revisions were not as wholesale, consisting mainly of typographical changes, changes of names and terms where their topicality made them unintelligible to the modern reader, changes of detail in keeping with his better understanding of aristocratic manners, and additions of historical and geographical addenda wherever such would clarify a point for the modern reader.

For this study I have chosen to quote from the collected edition begun in the 1930's. Obviously the *Standard Edition* of Shaw's works contains the most readily available of the editions, the earlier published editions being somewhat less available, and the original versions being scarce indeed. Further, as my purpose is to get people to read the novels, I can best serve that purpose by quoting from the edition that is not only the most available but also the best written. The later versions have the added advantage of better proving my thesis by showing us a Shaw more conscious of what the novels mean. Shaw's revisions of any significance are all in the direction of making more explicit the point that I consider central to my study of the novels. That is, his revisions do not change the meaning of the novels, they simply bring out that meaning more clearly.

Shaw tried his hand at another novel in 1887–88, but left it unfinished. His secretary dug it up late in Shaw's life, confronted him with the evidence of his own handwriting, and forced him to concede that he must have written it, although he had no memory of it. He allowed the fragment to be published posthumously (1958), rightly believing that he was near death, into which no critic could follow.

But for all practical purposes, Shaw's novel writing came to an end with the completion of *An Unsocial Socialist*. He claims that he gave up not so much because he was discouraged by lack of publication (indeed, the novels did a respectable business after he gave up novel writing and ceased to care about them), but because he was busy with something new. He had read Marx and George and become a Fabian. Fabianizing took a lot of his time. Furthermore, Marx had showed him the extent of his ignorance of the economic motive of society. Everything had to be re-learned. This was brought home to him when the attempt to write a Marxist interpretation of capitalist society broke down in "sheer ignorance," leaving us with only the first two chapters—*An Unsocial Socialist*. At this point Shaw left the society of his novels for the society of friends, Fabians, and Fabian friends. He spent the next decade establishing himself as a very social social-ist, before taking up playwriting with anything like serious in-tent.

Before beginning a close scrutiny of the novels, it might be salutary to recount an anecdote Shaw tells in his preface to *Cashel Byron's Profession*. It seems that when the novels were brought out in book editions around 1900, the American pub-lisher unwittingly confounded reviewing critics by inverting the order of their creation, publishing novel number five first, novel number four second, and so on. "Reviewers, unaware that the publisher was working backwards through the list, pointed out the marked advance in my style, the surer grip, the clearer form, the finer art, the maturer view of the world, and so forth."[3] The moral is plain, if painful to the trusting critic, and I shall try to keep it before me in the pages that follow.

3. Bernard Shaw, *Cashel Byron's Profession*, p. x.

The Art of the Novels

In writing about the art of Shaw's novels, the critic must be careful to do two things. First, he must ignore almost everything Shaw himself has said about the novels. Second, he must ignore almost everything the critics have said about the novels. At bottom they are the same thing, for what the critics had to say was largely what Shaw had put into their heads to say.

Robert Hogan, in the first really thoughtful and competen criticism ever to be published on the art of Shaw's novels, ha explained perfectly why the novels have met with very cavali treatment.[1] It seems Shaw himself is to blame for having misl his critics by commenting strategically rather than critical Shaw's actual fondness for the novels, says Hogan, "was te pered by an uneasy suspicion that others might think them worthy of a pre-eminent dramatist—mere apprentice work fact."[2] Further, because "his later work was so consistently universally successful . . . even the mature aplomb of a S might have felt uneasy about the consistent and universal f of his first work."[3] So, Hogan believes, Shaw set up "a s screen of bantering insouciance"[4] to disguise his diffiden viction that the novels were far from being inferior.

1. Some credit should also be given to Homer Woodbridge fine chapter on the novels in *George Bernard Shaw: Creative* Among manuscripts, Stanley Weintraub's "Bernard Shaw: N contains a fund of information on both the novels and the early Shaw, and John von Behren Rodenbeck's "Alliance and Misalliar Critical Study of Bernard Shaw's Novels" is a stimulating treatm the novels that includes many interesting comments on Shaw's man revisions. Perhaps I ought to point out here that the original vers my work was written in 1964, several months before Hogan's articl published and two years before I read Rodenbeck's dissertation. them a great deal in the revision of my manuscript, but it is a fact had arrived at many of the same conclusions independently.

2. Robert Hogan, "The Novels of Bernard Shaw," *English Liter* *in Transition 1880–1920*, p. 63.   3. *Ibid.*, p. 64.   4. *Ibid.*

The critics, largely biographers who give the impression of having merely skimmed through the novels, took Shaw's strategic comments as straightforward critical commentary. If the author was flippantly contemptuous of his early works, so too were the critics. If the author was facetious and superficial in his explanation of the novels' origins and intentions, the critics followed suit. In Hogan's words, "Shavian criticism has tended to accept Shaw's own simplified estimate of his work for the full and sober statement, just as people have tended to accept the Shavian mask for the real face. Behind Shaw's harlequin mask, however, was the face of a man of genius, compassion and, surprisingly, diffidence. Indeed, even in the apparently unbridled egotism of the self-advertisements, that curious diffidence kept rising to the surface."[5]

That curious diffidence misled his biographers, busy with other parts of that long and eventful life they were chronicling, into hasty readings of the novels and incautious acceptance of the critical clichés coined by Shaw himself. Archibald Henderson, Shaw's chief biographer, summarizes friendly critical opinion (prior to Hogan) when he writes that "Shaw's novels survive as a thin tail to his soaring dramatic kite; they are chiefly memorable as prentice tentatives, in an ill-chosen field, for works of genius in his true literary metier of the drama."[6] The metaphor of the kite would be all right if we were meant to understand by it that the kite cannot fly without the tail, but rather Henderson means to glorify Shaw's dramatic talents at the deprecation of his novels. This is the familiar pattern in Shaw criticism. Even more explicitly Henderson wrote: "Is Shaw a great novelist? Answer: a resounding No. His novels are amusing, eccentric, stilted, jejune, and filled with acute but inexpertly expressed observations on life and art and music and pugilism and marriage and society and Socialism. . . . Shaw was inexperienced and immature; and he lacked inside knowledge of, behind-the-scenes ac-

5. For samples of Shaw's contradictory remarks about the novels, see Hogan, p. 63.

6. Archibald Henderson, *George Bernard Shaw: Man of the Century*, p. 8.

quaintance with, the society and the individual social types of the period. Of his novels, he once remarked to me, with pawky humor: 'The best I can say of them is that neither Dickens nor Trollope could have written them.' "[7] To this Hogan cogently replies, "Mr. Henderson apparently did not realize that, despite the tone of rueful deprecation, the best that Shaw could say of the novels was that they were beyond the capabilities of two pre-eminent masters of English fiction."[8]

One could go on at great length quoting damaging comments on the novels, but they are all rather tiresomely the same, and our time could be better spent by simply accounting for them. Hogan sums up his introductory point by declaring the many condemnations "highly inaccurate—as if the critics had swallowed *in toto* Shaw's tongue in cheek deprecation of the novels, without having closely scrutinized the books themselves."[9] There is some excuse for their not having penetrated Shaw's "smokescreen," however, for it was a masterful disguise: "In later years, through his prefaces, Shaw perfected the pose of literary master of ceremonies who introduced and interpreted his own work. This practice was not so unfortunate when the work was a play which had finally to stand alone for judgment on the stage, but novels have no such separate life, and the diffident Shaw succeeded only too well in his diffident depreciations. When diffidence is cloaked in tones of fluently witty assurance, it is not too curious for that diffidence to be taken as aversion."[10]

The various charges against Shaw's novels take five main forms—that they are unreal in their portrayal of life, that they are stilted and unnatural in their language, that they are plotless, that they are inconsistent in their characterization, and that they are propagandistic, "talky," and often irrelevant in their detail. Robert Hogan has expertly refuted the first two charges, but the other three require a more elaborate and convincing refutation than anyone has given them.

According to Hogan, "the most damaging accusation leveled

7. Archibald Henderson, "Where Shaw Stands Today," *Bulletin of the Shaw Society of America*, p. 4.

8. Hogan, p. 64.   9. *Ibid.*   10. *Ibid.*

at Shaw's novels is probably Archibald Henderson's assertion
that Shaw did not know what he was writing about."[11] Each of
Shaw's novels is essentially a study of manners, and Henderson
argued that Shaw's knowledge of the society he was writing
about was too limited to enable him to create a convincing verisimilitude. As usual, Henderson got his argument from Shaw himself. In the preface to *The Irrational Knot* Shaw confessed that
his novel was indeed marred by a special ignorance of life. Upon
exporting himself from Dublin to London he was "in a condition
of extreme rawness and inexperience concerning the specifically
English side of the life with which the book pretends to deal."[12]
What he lacked, he says, was "the touch of the literary diner-
out."[13] Shaw seems to be damning himself here, but further in-
vestigation of the same preface reveals an equally spirited defense of the reality his novel creates. For one thing, he had a sort
of "backstairs knowledge" of high society due to his previous
position "in the office of an Irish gentleman who acted as land
agent and private banker for many persons of distinction"[14] and,
furthermore, "it is possible for a London author to dine out in
the highest circles for twenty years without learning as much
about the human frailties of his hosts as the family solicitor or
(in Ireland) the family land agent learns in twenty days; and
some of this knowledge inevitably reaches his clerks, especially
the clerk who keeps the cash, which was my particular depart-
ment."[15] Thus if the novels err in their portrayal of aristocratic
life, the error is not the very crucial one of idealizing that life,
but of merely missing its economic basis. As Shaw says, "If, as I
suspect, I failed to create a convincingly verisimilar atmosphere
of aristocracy, it was not because I had any illusions or igno-
rances as to the common humanity of the peerage, and not because I gave literary style to its conversation, but because, as I
had no money, I had to blind myself to its enormous importance,
with the result that I missed the point of view, and with it the
whole moral basis, of the class which rightly values money, and

11. *Ibid.*, p. 106.
12. Bernard Shaw, *The Irrational Knot*, p. v.
13. *Ibid.*, p. viii.   14. *Ibid.*, p. ix.   15. *Ibid.*

plenty of it, as the first condition of a bearable life."[16] But if Shaw's portrayal of aristocratic life is incomplete due to his ignorance of its moral basis, the same is true of the portrayals of Fielding, Austen, Dickens, and every other English author who wrote without knowledge of Marxian economics. Shaw's novels are not failures on that score, any more than are the novels of Fielding, Austen, and Dickens. On that point, they all stand or fall together.

Actually, Shaw's novels rather remarkably are less flawed in their portrayal of aristocracy than were most of his predecessors' and quite a few of his contemporaries'. As Hogan says, "the chief pitfall for the portrayer of high society is attributing to it an intelligence, a charm and a wit never seen on land or sea. This specious glamor pervades even the fumbling, if commercially successful, attempts of writers like Michael Arlen and Noel Coward. Shaw, even in his teens, was too perceptive to be so easily taken in, and he saw 'that the aristocratic profession has as few geniuses as any other profession.' "[17]

To conclude Hogan's argument on this point: "For our purposes, it is significant that Shaw did not finally attribute any lack of verisimilitude in the novels to either social ignorance or lack of artistry. The partial failure of the world he describes in the novels is, according to his view and mine, more philosophic or sociologic than it is artistic. Most of the masterworks of the world have taken, however, a similarly limited view. A work of art is a selection, a focusing upon a certain aspect of a subject."[18] In the sense that in his novels Shaw has created "one unified world, impelled by the same single view, discussed in the same single language," "a world that is inimitable, full and convincing,"[19] then, Hogan believes, the world of his novels is as real as anything in fiction.

The second of the five charges—that Shaw's language was

16. *Ibid.*, p. x.
17. Hogan, p. 107. Furthermore, portrayal of aristocratic life is not really a major element in Shaw's novels. Quite a few of the characters and settings are middle or lower class or Bohemian.
18. *Ibid.*, pp. 107–8.   19. *Ibid.*, p. 108.

stilted and unnatural—cannot be refuted on every page of every novel, but Hogan has summoned more than enough evidence to prove that the charge is very exaggerated, and in my discussion of *Immaturity* I will suggest that the charge is even irrelevant. Once again, the source of the charge is Shaw himself. "I can guarantee the propriety of my early style," said Shaw. "It was the last thing in correctness. . . . I resolved that I would write nothing that should not be intelligible to a foreigner with a dictionary, like the French of Voltaire; and I therefore avoided idiom."[20] Furthermore, "I had . . . the classical tradition which makes all the persons in a novel, except the comically vernacular ones, or the speakers of phonetically spelt dialect, utter themselves in the formal phrases and studied syntax of eighteenth century rhetoric. In short, I wrote in the style of Scott and Dickens; and as fashionable society then spoke and behaved, as it still does, in no style at all, my transcriptions of Oxford and Mayfair may nowadays suggest an unaccountable and ludicrous ignorance of a very superficial and accessible code of manners."[21] Shaw certainly has some excuse, then, in that the meticulous, pedantic style he used for aristocratic speech was the literary fashion of the day. In fiction, persons of quality were expected to speak a noble, decorous language that befitted their rank; only the lower classes were expected to reveal their depravity by a corrupt use of the language. Further, if the narrator himself presumed to be noble, his exposition and narrative line were also expected to walk on stilts.

In view of the powerful hold this vogue of artificial language had upon a long line of eminent English writers, the wonder is not that Shaw partially succumbed to it but that he so often escaped it. True enough that *Immaturity* is rather stiffly worded, even in exposition and in the dialogues of non-aristocratic characters, but by his second novel his language was increasingly vitalized by idiom (for an impressive listing of idiomatic expressions in *The Irrational Knot*, see Hogan, p. 65), and his sentence

20. *Immaturity,* p. xxxix. Succeeding references to *Immaturity* will be by parenthetical citations in the text.
21. *The Irrational Knot,* pp. viii–ix.

structure was considerably less periodic and predictable. By the time Shaw reached the fourth and fifth novels, his language had lost much of its formality, and seems by comparison with his contemporaries' astonishingly modern. (Consider that the following novels were written at approximately the same time as *Immaturity*: Henry James' *The Madonna of the Future,* Thomas Hardy's *The Return of the Native,* and George Meredith's *The Egoist.*[22]) I cannot think of a single contemporary novelist of the years 1879–83 whose language had so successfully escaped the formal demands of the day's rather starchy rhetorical patterns. Really, Shaw's novels are so shot through with idioms, colloquialisms, jargon, argot, and slang that, as Hogan says, "the inability of Shaw's perceptive critics to see the idioms on nearly every page of these books is high testimony to the hypnotic persuasiveness of Shaw, the creator of critical clichés."[23]

The other charges—that the novels are plotless, talky, propagandistic, often irrelevant in their detail, and inconsistent in their characterization—cannot be dealt with very convincingly in summary fashion. They can be refuted only through a close analysis of the novels. Someday, perhaps, when Shaw criticism is further along, an enlightened critic will write a substantial book restricted entirely to considerations of the novels' art; but for the present a shorter treatment will have to suffice, if I am ever to get on to my main argument. Thus I restrict myself to a thorough demonstration of only one novel, followed by brief comments on the art of the other four novels in their individual sections. But if I can prove that Shaw's first novel, *Immaturity,* is largely innocent of the charges against it, then the case for the other four should be easier to make. What is true for *Immaturity* is more or less true for the others.[24]

22. Incidentally, George Meredith as a reader for Chapman & Hall recommended that *Immaturity* be turned down. Not surprisingly Shaw considered Meredith's novels to be fifty years out of date the day they were written.

23. Hogan, p. 65.

24. I considered treating superficially all five novels in the space I give

Immaturity is divided into four books. The first book, entitled "Islington," deals with Robert Smith's adventures in a suburban lodging house. Here he encounters Harriet Russell, a dressmaker and orphaned Scotchwoman befriended by Smith's landlady, Mrs. Froster. Harriet's practicality and common sense are important to Smith's appreciation of those virtues, but the book ends with a rather cool flirtation being disrupted by Harriet's removal to another residence, caused partly by the sale and impending demolition of Mrs. Froster's house. The second book, entitled "Aesthetics," takes place mostly at Perspective Park in Richmond, the estate of a wealthy would-be patron of the arts, Halket Grosvenor, who conducts a semi-bohemian open house for poets, painters, and musicians. Harriet's aunt being an employee at Perspective causes Harriet to set up shop nearby. Soon a promising young painter, Cyril Scott, makes Harriet's acquaintance and becomes infatuated with her. Meanwhile Smith has changed residence and become secretary for an Irish member of Parliament, Mr. Woodward. Scenes dealing with the life of Smith alternate with scenes at Perspective. The connection is made by Mr. Woodward's daughter, Isabella, a practiced flirt who maneuvers for the attentions of Cyril Scott. The third book is entitled "Courtship and Marriage," the courtship and marriage being that of Harriet Russell and Cyril Scott. Smith serves as witness and then makes his first acquaintance with Perspective society when he attends a recital by the poet Hawkshaw, friend of Cyril Scott. In the fourth book, entitled "Flirtation," Smith becomes involved in a triangle with Isabella and Hawkshaw, confounding Hawkshaw with his probity and disillusioning Isabella by his thoroughly upright behavior, on the one hand, and, on the other, by his rationalistic criticism of her cherished Catholicism. After the triangle breaks up, the book ends with Smith's decision to go into the civil service, for lack of anything better to do, and a diagnosis of Smith's immaturity by a now matronly Harriet.

---

to one, but I reminded myself that there are already plenty of superficial treatments available in print, if that is what one wants. It seemed to me that what I wanted and what Shaw scholarship needs is a move from the superficial to the thorough, from the impressionistic to the closely read.

In 1901, thirty years before *Immaturity* was published, Shaw remarked that even the mice hadn't been able to finish the manuscript of his first novel.[25] Evidently the readers for the many publishing houses in America and England who had been assigned the task of reviewing it managed to finish it well enough, only being prevented by their cultivated Victorian tastes from adequately digesting it. The reader for Macmillan expresses the universal dyspepsia: "I have given more than usual attention to this M.S., for it has a certain quality about it—not exactly of an attractive kind, but still not common. It is the work of a humourist and a realist, crossed, however, by veins of merely literary discussion. There is a piquant oddity about the situation now and then: and the characters are certainly not drawn after the conventional patterns of fiction. It is dry and ironic in flavor. . . . Recognizing all these things, I ask myself what it is all about; what is the key, the purpose, the meaning of a long work of this kind *without plot or issue.* . . . It is undoubtedly clever, but most readers would find it dry, unattractive, and *too devoid of any sort of emotion.* And then it is very long" (italics added).[26]

It is not surprising that the Victorian reader missed the point of the novel, for it was not a Victorian point. The book is about a new spirit rising out of the Victorian ethos, as yet largely unaware of its own character, only aware of being lost, misplaced, or unrealized, and of finding itself in rebellion against the standards of the day. It is a sign of the complacent times that the educated Victorian declared the most significant issue of the late nineteenth century—namely, the clash between the "Victorian" and the "modern"—to be no issue at all, thinking that a book pregnant with meaning was sterile of meaning.

The Macmillan reader, further, found the novel dry and without emotion—a criticism that would plague Shaw for the rest of his life. Certainly anyone who has spent much time wallowing in the salt sea of Victorian sentimentalism will find Shaw dry. But now that the classical spirit has re-emerged in modern literature, after the melancholy, long, withdrawing roar of the Victorian

25. *Cashel Byron's Profession*, p. ix.
26. Charles Morgan, *House of Macmillan, 1843–1943*, p. 119.

sea of sentimentalism, it is possible to return to Shaw's novels with the understanding that emotion does not have to drip or gush from the page in order to be called emotion. Dryness, we have relearned, is itself a way of expressing emotion. Shaw was using the "objective correlative" long before that term appeared in criticism. The following scene, appearing at the end of Book I, perfectly illustrates the excellent control of the young author over the emotional charge inherent in his material. Robert Smith has taken Harriet Russell to the railway station for her removal to Richmond from the lodging house in Islington they have both been living and romancing in. He "was surpised to find tears in his eyes" at their parting, and once again sees all the "occult charm" in her bearing that he had come to regard as a romantic delusion. After leaving her on the train, "he strolled away, noticing the grime of the station, and wondering how long it would take a single man to clean it. He endeavored to dismiss this impertinent idea, partly because he wanted to think about the dressmaker, and partly lest it should recur to him in a nightmare. But it would not be dismissed; for he thought of nothing else than of giddily swinging on a ladder among the sooty girders, trying to clean them with a towel and a small basin of water, until he reached Dodd's Buildings" (p. 97). As his only real friend abandons him, young Smith can think of nothing but the prodigious and giddy task of cleaning up the grime of the world in solitary effort. The presence of such objectification of emotion should have informed the Macmillan reader that Shaw's classical art was far from being emotionless, but critics of that age were apparently so blinded by their sentimentalist bias that they could not see any emotion that was not profuse and labeled. T. S. Eliot's reminder to critics about the "objective correlative" was, it seems, most opportune.

The Macmillan reader was equally obtuse in his notion that the novel was without plot. Many Victorian critics, as we now realize, had decided that there was only one sort of plot, the sort of mechanical contraption that Fielding and Dickens and many lesser writers often used to tease their readers into reading further, and it didn't seem to matter to those critics that, by their definition, a great deal of the world's best fiction was left plot-less.[27] If, however, plot is understood as a significant ordering of events and actions in a story to convey a dominant theme, then Shaw's novels, as well as Homer's epics, have plots.

Robert Hogan describes the plot of *Immaturity* as Chekhovian: "In the really accomplished uses of this structure, the various tales are intertwined with much dexterity and subtlety of effect. An author like Chekhov, or even a film director like D. W. Griffith in his movie *Intolerance,* will move rapidly and bewilder-ingly back and forth among the various strands of his plot, ever twisting them into a more cohesive unity by ironic juxtapositions and parallels. The final effect is rather like a half dozen vari-colored strands being so delicately meshed together that the ultimate rope appears an integral one-colored unity of rare excellence."[28] Hogan believes, however, that Shaw's use of the Chekhovian pattern was not entirely successful: "Shaw's 'rope' appears, by contrast, formed by cutting the individual strands into long lengths and knotting one strand to another almost at random. This handling of the structure seems arbitrarily episodic rather than coherently meaningful, and this inchoate impression is further confused by several purely illustrative incidents in-truded throughout the books, as well as by a number of ensemble scenes which predictably lack the cumulative irony of such scenes in a Chekhov play."[29]

While I agree that the plot structure of *Immaturity* seems rather Chekhovian at times and that it is not entirely successful at this, I find it less "arbitrarily episodic" and more "coherently meaningful" than Hogan does. Our disagreement arises from a different reading of the story. There is much to be said for the plot's being Chekhovian, as the novel does indeed present "a comprehensive satire upon the totality of a society,"[30] but Hogan

27. For Shaw's own description of this sort of plot, see the section "A Monster of the Body," note 8.

28. Hogan, p. 67.

29. *Ibid.* Rodenbeck, however, would call the plot Mozartian. See his ingenious comparison of *Immaturity* to *Don Giovanni* in the first chapter of his dissertation.

30. Hogan, p. 67.

seems to miss the more basic and more conventional *Bildungs-roman* structure that underlies the apparent Chekhovianism of the novel. I think that Shaw was more intent on writing a conventional novel for his first venture into literature than Hogan supposes. Shaw's most immediate literary model was the very popular *Bildungsroman* of Charles Dickens. As in *Great Expectations,* the *Bildungsroman* is a "long, developmental novel, in which a young man serves his apprenticeship to life with its attendant failures and successes, to end up a wiser man."[31] It is "necessarily episodic—the structure of the novel follows a long development from childhood through success or failure, scene following scene in chronological order."[32] True enough that *Immaturity* does not follow the life of its hero from wretched childhood to successful adulthood, yet it does portray the more modest progression of a significant part of that life in chronological order in the *Bildungsroman* manner.[33] While the plot of *Immaturity* may be a hybrid, partly Chekhovian in its ironic counterpointing, the *Bildungsroman* pattern is surely more basic to the novel's structure.[34]

31. Frederick R. Karl, *The Contemporary English Novel,* p. 16.

32. *Ibid.*

33. More accurately, perhaps *Immaturity* should be classified as a *Künstlerroman,* which focuses specifically on the development of an artist.

34. Years later, in *Pen Portraits and Reviews,* p. 22, Shaw "held . . . that a play is a vital growth and not a mechanical construction; that a plot is the ruin of a story and therefore of a play, which is essentially a story . . . in short, that a play should never have a plot, because, if it has any natural life in it, it will construct itself, like a flowering plant, far more wonderfully than its author can consciously construct it." Such quotations point to Shaw's inclinations for Romantic theory, but Shaw's practice as a novelist and a playwright reveal even deeper allegiances to classical methods. Although his novels and plays are almost always personal and expressive, and his constant theme is the Romantic one of genius in conflict with system, Shaw did not use the Romantic instrument of the confessional novel, nor did he realize the Romantic doctrine of following the motions of the mind with such startling Joycean innovations as internal monologue. Even had the Joycean method occurred to Shaw, he probably would not have used it because of his deeply ingrained habit of representing reality in literature externally, by means of surface char-

Hogan arrives at his opinion by concluding that "Robert Smith is not the book's dominating character,"[35] and I arrive at my opinion by concluding that Smith most certainly is the book's dominating character and, further, that the story is told primarily for his sake. Hogan is correct that Smith is too often missing from the narrative to make the novel a pure *Bildungsroman,* yet Hogan does not consider the possibility that the scenes from which Smith is absent are told for the sake of further characterizing the absent Smith by way of ironic contrast. A possible misunder-standing of Shaw's technique is pointed to, I think, in the follow-ing insightful comment of William Irvine on the genesis of *Immaturity:* "Shaw was probably worried about London, too. Like most puritans, he was acutely conscious of the integrity and importance of his own individual soul. In the midst of so much indifferent humanity, of so much irrelevant striving and working and succeeding and failing, the clear, sharp contours of the mind and personality of Bernard Shaw grew a little vague, even a little insignificant. Surely a 350-page definition of that fanatically honest and independent individual would be ex-tremely valuable. To write a novel was obviously a duty of spiritual clarification. This book was finished in 1879."[36] Despite the sarcasm, the queer use of the term "puritan," and the ten-dency to forget Shaw's ironic handling of Smith, Irvine was acute enough to see that the novel was an attempt at self-definition; unfortunately, the rest of Irvine's comments on the novel reveal that he is generally oblivious to Shaw's technique of defining himself in relation to others. When the novel's hero is off the page, Irvine is often unable to see the relevance of the novel. It is to Hogan's credit that he can see the relevance of scenes from

acter, surface action, and objective correlative, supplemented by the objective analysis of the omniscient author. In theme and inclination Shaw may have been Romantic, but in habit he was thoroughly classical. You will not find in Shaw any subjective presentations of the poet's mind (through the use of first person narrative), let alone any confessions of the poet's mind; rather you will find the poet's mind expressing itself by projecting into surface reality, in the classical manner.

35. Hogan, p. 66.
36. William Irvine, *The Universe of G. B. S.,* p. 21.

which Smith is absent to the total thematic intention of the novel,
but he does not see that these scenes are relevant not only to the
novel's theme but also to the novel's central action, the defining
of the hero. Everything that happens in *Immaturity* happens, for
one reason, because it contributes to the identification of Robert
Smith.

It is in the Huxley-like orchestration of the Perspective scenes,
from all but the last of which Smith is absent, that the novel is
most vulnerable to the criticism of relevance. Do the many dis-
cussions of art and life in this section take place merely because
the twenty-three-year-old author felt like voicing his current
opinions on such subjects, or because they are an integral part of
the novel's art? William Irvine complains of these scenes that
"the characters utter rationalistic opinions on philosophy, ethics,
religion, literature, music, painting, and take a weighty interest
in nearly everything except in getting on with the story."[37]
Irvine, in short, is accusing Shaw of abandoning the novel for
the sake of reviewing his own weighty opinions on art and life
by using the Perspective characters as his mouthpieces.

But Irvine, indulging in a familiar vice of Shaw critics, does
not consider the fact that the opinions uttered by the characters
are perfectly in keeping with their very different characters and
develop even further their characterization. More importantly,
Irvine does not seem to notice that the reader is considerably
clearer about the artistic temperament of Smith because it has
been put in ironic juxtaposition with the temperaments to be
found at Perspective. That is why Shaw used the pattern of alternating scenes, a scene at Perspective followed by a scene dealing
with Smith. This is not just a way of keeping up with two different stories that will eventually intersect; rather a great irony
cumulates as each scene dealing with the separate life of Smith
reflects upon the group scenes at Perspective, as the life of a true
artist reflects upon the lives of false artists. The two alternating
themes are brought into rather discordant conjunction at the
esthetically right moment, near the end of the third book, just before Smith meets Perspective society, when Smith witnesses the

37. *Ibid.*, p. 23.

marriage of Harriet Russell and Cyril Scott, the marriage of sense and sensibility. This marriage, struggling for realization within the psyche of Robert Smith as well, is a marriage that makes Mr. and Mrs. Scott feel foreign to Perspective, just as Smith feels foreign to it. Perspective is no more the proper lodging house for the true artist than Islington is for the true man, nor is Grosvenor as landlord an improvement over Mrs. Froster as landlady.[38]

The Perspective scenes are, further, relevant to the novel's central theme—the theme of immaturity. As Hogan says, *Immaturity* presents "a comprehensive gallery of immaturities. . . . Shaw is quite as concerned with the immaturity of Cyril Scott the painter, or Hawkshaw the poet, or Fenwick the wastrel, or Davis the brooding preacher, or Isabella Woodward the flirt, or mousey Fanny Watkins the shopkeeper's daughter, as he is with that of Smith."[39] I would only add that Shaw is interested in the immaturities of the others principally because they help to define the immaturity of Smith. Smith's immaturity is not of the usual sort, Shaw is saying. To continue with Hogan's point:

> Actually, Shaw devotes much space and "plot" to his minor adult characters, and he apparently is showing that these characters are quite as immature as the young principals. Woodward, the Irish peer, possesses a clear practicality about some personal matters, but is hopelessly muddled in business and uninformed about Irish politics. Halket Grosvenor, the "munificent patron and hospitable entertainer of artists of all denominations," is almost totally lacking in taste and perception, and art is to him a toy valued primarily for its social prestige. Even Lady Geraldine Porter, one of the more perceptive older people, fribbles her life away by visiting her friends and by arranging artistic afternoons of an inanely frivolous character. Mrs. Froster, Smith's quondam landlady, in one scene throws a tantrum which

---

38. Perspective is perhaps thematically connected with Islington by being a lodging house for artists, although aristocratically free of charge.
39. Hogan, p. 66.

reduces her to tears. In another scene, Smith intervenes to
save another landlady whom her husband is smashing over
the head with an iron skillet. That lady immediately turns
on Smith, and, in petulant outrage, denounces him for interfering. Mrs. Watkins, Fanny's mother, is a foolish and
irritable domestic tyrant who must be coddled out of the
sulks by her husband and daughter. Indeed, there are so
many minor as well as major instances of immaturity—in
art, in politics, in religion, in domestic life—that Shaw's
purpose seems quite emphatically the revelation that society, in all levels and classes, is hopelessly, helplessly and
irretrievably immature.[40]

To Hogan's point I would add my own point that none of the
above immaturities are committed by Robert Smith, for his immaturity is of a special sort, perhaps best understood as a reaction
against all of the other immaturities.

Rodenbeck has noticed too that *Immaturity* perfectly exem-
plifies the "posture of opposition" fundamental to Shavian
heroes. "*Immaturity* supplies us with a kind of fundamental
Shaw, a Shaw without the 'ideas' that so many critics find either
confusing or annoying, a Shaw in which we can see the posture
of opposition clearly operating as a motiveless attitude."[41] This
novel, says Rodenbeck, proves that the code of beliefs critics
have come to associate with Shaw (Creative Evolution and
Socialism) were preceded by an almost pure negativism. The

40. *Ibid.,* pp. 66–67.
41. Rodenbeck, p. v. See Rodenbeck, pp. 24–30, for an interesting
comparison of Smith to the traditional hero of ironic comedy, the *Phar-
makos,* who as a *Neinsager* either analyzes, condemns, and repudiates the
vices of a sinful society or suffers as the victim of the same vices. The
expression "posture of opposition" Rodenbeck derives from Richard M.
Ohmann's excellent study of Shaw's expository prose style, *Shaw: The
Style and the Man,* p. 107. Shaw was such a rebel, says Ohmann, that "the
habit of saying No seems to have a life of its own in Shaw's style, over
and above its utility." Ohmann suspects that the posture of denial precedes Shaw's code of beliefs, and a study of *Immaturity* certainly bears
him out.

typical Shavian hero of the novels discovers himself in an environment that he does not like, but immaturely can think of
nothing better to do than priggishly oppose its values. Not until
the last novel, *An Unsocial Socialist,* will the hero possess anything like a positive program. For the moment he can only say
No in thunder. (More precisely, the "No in thunder" will come
from the hero of the third novel, Owen Jack. Robert Smith is too
shy to do anything more than argue a bit, look scornful, and
shake his head, and Edward Conolly, the hero of the second
novel, is too coolly civilized to do anything more than argue in a
rational manner against the falsity of the day. But they all share
the negative, rebellious attitude of the Shavian hero.)

St. John Davis, a tubercular evangelist who is ruined by his
obsession for Harriet Russell, is a perfect example of a character
who exists principally to define the immaturity of Smith as a reaction against the immaturities of Victorian society.[42] One
Christmas day Smith adventures into one of Davis' revival meetings, at which Smith is handed some tracts that "he found neither
credible, Christian, nor interesting" (p. 19). As he is musically
inclined, he cannot resist joining in the hymn singing ("We will
all be happy over there"), but he is vastly amused by a young
man, "earnest and proud of his oratory, who offered up a long
prayer, in the course of which he suggested such modifications of
the laws of nature as would bring the arrangement of the universe into conformity with his own tenets" (p. 20). Finally, when
Davis gives a very affective peroration on his nearness to death
and his trust in the Greater Physician to reward him with celes-
tial good health for his perseverance in his evangelistic duties,
there is much weeping and wringing of hands, but Smith "proud
of his cynicism . . . looked as scornful as he could" (p. 20). The
function of Davis, then, is obviously to further the definition of
Smith as sophomoric intellectual. The tone of Shaw's narration
makes it quite plain that while he considers this example of Victorian religion to be extremely foolish and immature, it is no more
so than the priggish young hero who scorns it. Smith, like so

42. Typical of the critical myopia that has missed the art of Shaw's
novels is Woodbridge's statement that Davis has "no real function," p. 7.

many young people who are repelled by the falsity of social and religious convention, confuses being rational with being wise. Seemingly a reaction against a hypocritically pious upbringing, Smith's rationalism combatively declares its agnosticism and in-sists that churches are abodes of barbarous superstition. That this immaturity does not much improve in the course of the novel is proved by Smith's reaction in the fourth book to the Catholi-cism of Isabella. He dismisses her church as an "ecstasy shop," and after a lively debate with her on the subject of religion, he "strode home, excited by his hatred of religion, puffed up by the success of his legitimate priggishness, and amusing himself with visions of destroyed Churches and confuted priests" (p. 376).

The typical path of Smith's sort of immaturity is from disgust with the real to infatuation with the ideal. After extensive read-ing in the works of such lofty souls as Ruskin, Mill, and Shelley, Smith "became intolerant of everything that fell short of his highest ideal of beauty and power. . . . He planned an austere religion for the worship of Truth; and made an attempt to be-come a vegetarian, which was frustrated in three days by the inability of Rose [the servant] to vary a regimen of boiled cab-bage. He was credulous when a reformer pointed out abuses, and skeptical when a conservative defended institutions" (pp. 54–55). In short, the young Shaw writes, in merciless summa-tion of his previous immaturity, Smith was in that phase of devel-opment "in which acute perception, hatred of falsehood, love of liberty, pregnant truths, and scrupulous purity, are complicated with mental color blindness, unconscious sophistry, intolerance, platitudes, and subtle epicureanism. Being through the defective induction of inexperience unable to discriminate accurately the natural from the accidental, he acquired that fine instinct for the prettiest half of the truth which makes young men thorough in partisanship only" (p. 55).

If Smith is immature in the manner of his rebellion from so-ciety, nevertheless, the principal blame for his alienation lies upon society itself. Shaw makes this point in many ways, but especially effective is his use of setting. The novel begins with Smith's search for lodgings in Islington, a place in London. This setting is symbolic, as well as actual. Islington, more than just a place in London, is a state of mind. It is the Victorian thing itself. The part of it that Smith chose for his lodging was called "Dodd's Buildings," a smallish square containing "eleven severely re-spectable houses. It was a quiet spot in a noisy neighborhood, and conveyed an impression that Dodd, though unimaginative as an architect, was a strictly pious man" (p. 3). Smith's knock at the door of Number 3 causes an ancient, and yet very Victorian, sound—the scream of the mistress of the house at the servant to answer the door. Rose, the servant, is characteristically in no hurry. When a boarder complains of the knocking, Mrs. Froster retorts, "And do you expect me to take my servant's place, Mr. Fenwick?" (p. 3). Mrs. Froster is more subdued upon noticing that the visitor is a gentleman, but she quickly lets her new lodger know of Rose's stubborn pride which will go before her fall. "There is a wicked devil in her. I have spoken to the minister about her" (p. 4), explains Mrs. Froster, unintentionally ex-plaining more about respectable, caste-ridden Victorian England than about wicked Rose. For what could be more childish and more foolish than a system of caste that makes the purely func-tional opening of a door a matter of grave ceremony? Smith simply wants the door opened, and if he becomes impatient with a way of life that makes the opening of that door an issue of morality, we can hardly be surprised.

Later Smith is invited into the front drawing room, "Mrs. Froster's room of state, which she never let" (p. 24). It seems Mrs. Froster (the name is indicative of respectability's habitual temperature) keeps her best for her room of state. Shaw enjoys describing it: "The table was walnut, and was covered with a crimson cloth, in the centre of which a case of stuffed birds stood on a Berlin wool mat. On the mantelpiece were an ornamental clock, a velvet watch-stand, and two plaster of Paris vases under glass shades. A convex mirror, encircled by a gilt frame of ear-nestly ugly design, hung on the wall opposite the pier glass. The window was draped with red damask curtains, which contrasted with the green Venetian blind; and the appearance of the whole room was worthy of the gentility to which, through many years

of struggling, Mrs. Froster had never relinquished her pretension" (p. 24). Shaw's "earnestly ugly" describes the respectable
Victorian way of life with perfect fitness. It is this earnest and
ugly Islington that is to be Smith's home, "but the reflection that
this was to be his home struck cold to the heart of the tenant"
(p. 4).

Smith is further chilled by the ugliness of Mrs. Froster's relationship with her servant and her other male roomer, Fraser Fenwick, a down-at-heels gentleman. When Smith is served tea,
Rose handles "her mistress's china as if it was her mistress's
head" (p. 7), then descends the stairs for a shrill argument.
Shortly after, Mrs. Froster hastens up the stairs to engage the
deadbeat Fenwick in battle, the unholy noise of which penetrates
the floor of Smith's room. This is followed by a visit from Fenwick himself, who makes himself so disagreeable that Smith is
saved from resigning his lodging only by the opportune entrance
of the intriguing Harriet Russell. The principal point of this
scene is the contrast between Mrs. Froster's pretensions of propriety and gentility and the vital, ugly, and businesslike way she
runs her house.

Thus in placing Smith in the Islington lodging house, Shaw
expertly sets the stage for both Smith's rebellion and a comprehensive satire upon the whole of society. Among all the symbols
of the Victorian age that have appeared in fiction, Shaw's Islington lodging house is a worthy member. The lodging house implies
that respectability is in business for itself, whatever its pretension. Being the morality of the middle class, respectability always
has rooms to let, mostly to would-be gentlemen. Roomers come
and go, signifying the impermanence of this way of life. The
House of Respectability is a midway stopping point for those on
the way up (Smith) or down (Fenwick), to the places above or
below where one can be comfortably well-bred or ill-bred, which-
ever the case may be. Being the straight chair for curved spines
that it is, respectability is always rather uncomfortable for the
social traveler. The trueborn aristocrat or proletarian can relax
in the assurance that he is in his place, but the rising bourgeois or
the down-at-heels gentleman realizes that he is no place at all,

merely renting a temporary room, and must conform to the shape of his landlady's morality just as his spine conforms to the shape of her furniture. The House of Respectability is always more like an institution of spinal correction than a home. Small wonder then that Smith discovers in Islington that a house is not a home, and small wonder that he rebels against the unnatural constrictions of the respectable way of life.

One of the important actions of *Immaturity* is that of people finding their level. Fraser Fenwick, for instance, discovers by the end of the novel that he belongs in a class below his birth, that he is not the born aristocrat he thinks he is but a born shopkeeper. However, it takes him a long, painful, and embarrassing time to discover this. His function in the novel is largely to help define the term "gentleman" by being so obviously not a gentleman. Fenwick is all pride. Dissolute habits have caused him to fall from the pampered position of his early childhood (he had been raised by Lady Geraldine Porter, a frequenter of Perspective), and now he struggles to keep up the pretensions of refined gentility. Engaged to a Miss Fanny Watkins, a pious if somewhat rebellious daughter of a merchant, Fenwick is so haughtily class conscious in his dealings with her family that the rubbing together of aristocratic and mercantile class pretensions produces an abrasive comedy of manners. Fanny's parents are as determined to deflate Fenwick's aristocratic ego as Fenwick is to assert his precedence. Mrs. Watkins especially is "not a woman to be trifled with," and her own rigid code of respectability makes Fenwick extremely uncomfortable in his genteel shabbiness. Thus the false pride of Fenwick is contrasted with the more natural and unaffected gentility of Smith. Smith is not above a bit of snobbishness now and then,[43] but in contrast to the childish posings of Fenwick his behavior seems rather adult.

43. Although Smith has many superior instincts, he has contracted a few inferior habits, such as his snobbishness. He is consoled by the smallness of his pay at Figgis & Weaver because it is at least a wholesale business, the vulgar retail trade being beneath him (p. 11). When Davis gives him some sound advice, Smith refuses to listen because "he could not believe that a man who dropped his aitches could have anything to teach

Though immature in the manner of his rebellion, Smith is quite justified in opposing the immaturities of Victorian society. But his rebellion poses a question—namely, if a very intelligent and sociable young man like Smith finds himself opposed to most of the social norms of the day, and because of his opposition finds himself in danger of ostracism at the worst and social disapproval at the least, what can he do to remove the opposition and continue as a functioning member of the social group? One answer, apparently, is that he can teach. He can rejoin the group by educating them in a way of living more acceptable to himself. It is for this reason that the Shavian hero is so often an arguer. As Rodenbeck says, "Shaw's problem . . . was to create characters who would be arguers, characters who would embody his posture of opposition, his rebellion, and at the same time stay within the realm of the thing they oppose and rebel against long enough to conduct an argument."[44] If in *Immaturity* the principal (i.e., Aristotelian) action is the hero's search for identity, one of the major devices in this search is that of argument. Smith discovers who he is by attempting to teach others. His arguments with the conventions of religion, gentility, and art reveal to him by contrast what he is, at the same time as they strive to convert others to his way of life.

Significantly, of all the people available for instruction Smith picks Harriet Russell as his special pupil, thus establishing a

---

him. He was only eighteen" (p. 22). Smith took the job with Woodward because, among other reasons, "Queen's Gate was a more refined sphere than the City. This last consideration was decisive" (p. 173). When Woodward's butler tries to be familiar with his employer's new secretary, Smith "desiring to maintain a distance between them," responds coolly (p. 180). Later, after describing Harriet to Isabella, he is asked if he is related to Harriet in any way. At first Smith vigorously denies any relation, "discovering by his feelings at this question that he was not so thorough a republican as he had believed himself to be" (p. 223). Obviously Smith was trained in snobbery, whoever his parents were, and his republican principles are sometimes overpowered by his aristocratic habits. Perhaps one of the chief signs of immaturity is the inability to act independently of the habits inculcated by parents.

44. Rodenbeck, p. vii.

pattern and a relationship that shall recur many times in Shaw's career. Harriet is proto-Candida–Ann Whitefield to this proto-Marchbanks–John Tanner. She is the Philistine female, as described by Shaw in *The Quintessence of Ibsenism,* to whom the Artist-Philosopher seems fatally attracted. The attraction is immediately physical, for Smith much admires Harriet's "extraordinary grace of movement and self-possession of manner" (pp. 12–13); he is "fascinated by the sweetness of her smile, and awed by the impression of power which he received from her fine strong hands and firm jaw" (p. 13). He was accustomed to seeing women "walk like parrots," but Harriet moved "with the grace of a lioness" (p. 13). She would be "poetry personified," thinks Smith, if only she were "conscious of her unaccountable grace" (p. 54).

If the attraction were merely physical, however, it is doubtful that the intellectual Smith would have attempted Harriet's education. He sees immediately that as her body is already more "educated" than his ever will be, if he is to teach her anything the lessons must aim at the mind. He is encouraged to pursue her education by her eagerness for knowledge and her unusual reasonableness of mind. His own rationalism seems to have something in common with Harriet's common sense in their mutual scorn of superstition. Harriet never goes to prayer meetings, Smith discovers from Mrs. Froster, because she had been brought up by her father "to believe that there is no good in such things" (p. 26). Mrs. Froster had been scandalized by Mr. Russell's refusal to send Harriet to school "for fear she would be taught to read the Book of Books, where he said she would find nothing but bad examples" (p. 28). Mr. Russell had told his daughter, "When you want to do whats right, youll see your way straight enough without the help of religion. When you dont, youll easily be able to invent as good an excuse as youll find in the Bible" (p. 28). While he lived, Mr. Russell brought Harriet up in the liberal tradition, allowing her to "go where she likes, except to church; and say what she likes, except her prayers" (p. 29). To all this Smith can heartily concur, for he believes that "the majority of prayers are very little else than wishes" (p. 23).

Unfortunately this apparent sympathy of minds leads Smith to misunderstand the nature of Harriet's mind. He does not notice at first that while his own position of rationalistic skepticism has been arrived at independently, the result of a logical-minded consideration of the discrepancy between religion's theory and religion's practice, Harriet has acquired her skepticism as a family inheritance from her father, however much her own practical, worldly sense reinforces it. It is therefore doubtful that Harriet would have arrived at this position on her own, as she is otherwise quite conventional in her opinions. Had she been born in a more conventionally religious environment, her opinion of religion would have sounded a good deal more like Mrs. Froster's than Smith's. The Philistine, Shaw insisted, was characterized mainly by a rather easy-going, complacent acceptance of established institutions, especially the institution of marriage. For instance, when Smith timidly shows Harriet his rather florid sonnet entitled "Lines to a Southern Passion Flower," inspired by a local ballet dancer, Harriet's reaction is as frosty as Mrs. Froster's would be. She is "sure that no woman who respected herself would . . . [dance] before a crowd of people without being decently dressed" (p. 82).

Smith gets a good view of Harriet's limitations when he attempts to teach her French and to start her reading books. She wants to learn French for business purposes, of course, and is disturbed by how affected it sounds when Smith pronounces it. She has a capricious memory, and Smith is confounded by its contradictions until he discovers "that she remembered perfectly all that he told her, and forgot all that she read. He found her quick to seize isolated explanations and impenetrably stupid when he endeavored to make her see analogies in the construction of the language, which he had a pedantic taste for drawing" (p. 52). When he tries to get her reading books, he finds to his dismay that her tastes are confined to romantic fiction and descriptive travel. She returned his precious Shelley as " ' a good book, only fit for children.' In revenge, he gave her Robinson Crusoe; and she, quite unconscious of the sarcasm, not only read it diligently, but contended for the truth of the narrative afterwards in an animated discussion with him. Struck by this, he followed it up with The Pilgrim's Progress, which she accepted with bad grace as having 'good' characteristics, but finished nevertheless. The Vicar of Wakefield finally convinced her that reading was a pleasure, she having before considered it an irk-some educational process" (p. 56).

The gap between Smith and Harriet widens the further they venture into the world of intellect. Smith is tremendously trans-formed by the educational process, acquiring an ever subtler insight into human nature, but "meanwhile Miss Russell seemed to remain stationary" (p. 55). She became acquainted with new facts, but did not assimilate them. "Her new accomplishments, instead of changing her position in relation to the world, seemed to attach themselves externally to her, as barnacles do to a ship" (p. 55). Her refusal or inability to budge an intellectual inch is the despair of the rapidly changing Smith. He "was constantly puzzled by the contrast between her shrewdness and her simplic-ity. She looked on him as a very great scholar; but her admiration of his learning was tempered by doubts whether he did not know more than was good for him. She appreciated his intellectuality and freedom from vulgarity. Still, she could not believe in the real worth of attainments which left their possessor with an income and position no better than that of many ignorant persons. . . . She felt sure that he was wrong and the world right in most of their differences . . . being an ambitious utilitarian of strong pur-pose, and little sentiment, she held him in a regard which partook . . . of that pity which is akin to contempt" (pp. 56–57).

Thus it is that Shaw makes Smith understand the difference between his own quality of mind and the mind of the vast major-ity of human beings. Harriet may be "poetry personified" in the body, but in the mind she is limited by the scope of the practical. This is artfully conveyed by the image of Harriet at the sewing machine. Smith comes to enjoy the sound of the rattling machine, for it keeps him company, as perhaps the vision of Penelope at the loom would comfort a wandering Odysseus. Further, the sound of the machine is the sound of industry, of commitment to a practical task, and to the professionally uncommitted Smith it might have sounded like music. But, gradually, the sound of dedicated practicality Smith conceives to be a limitation. He discovers that Harriet lacks artistic sensibility. "That is the most insensible woman I ever saw. I believe she has no soul" (p. 54).

Harriet as Earth Mother—commonsensical, practical, and productive—forces Smith into a typical Shavian dilemma. Shaw knew, apparently at a very early age, that the skylarking intellectual must flirt with the Earth occasionally if he is to retain his sanity and his inspiration. After all, it is often of the Earth ("poetry personified") the skylark sings. Shaw was one blithe spirit who recognized the need to emotionalize his mental life by occasional contact with the sympathetic Earth. ("The attraction of the dancer made Smith feel that philosophy grew monotonous if not relieved by what he called a little flesh and blood, a phrase which means, according to the nature of the individual using it, a great deal of gross sensuality, or a snatch of innocent folly" [p. 83].) For Shaw the contact need involve no more than writing a letter to Ellen Terry or Stella Campbell, but at least he understood that the high and dry intellect soon withered away if it did not occasionally put down "roots" (not necessarily Freudian) into the soil of flesh-and-blood reality. Now the trouble with the Earth is that she is woefully limited in her appreciation of the intellectual virtues, generally pooh-poohing the Artist-Philosopher's vision of Ultimate Reality, and would ground the skylark for life if she had her way. Shaw himself guarded against a complete grounding by making his relations with the Earth of the flirtatious sort. Significantly, the last book of *Immaturity* is entitled "Flirtation," the "Courtship and Marriage" being subordinated to a less climactic position in the third book.

The metaphor of the skylark, however, is rather misleading. Certainly it misleads Harriet in her estimation of Smith. In contrasting the ingredients of Smith's personality with those of Scott, she decides in favor of Scott. She "admired [Scott] ardently. He seemed to her thoroughly a man, susceptible, intense, and altogether different from the pale scholar of Islington, whose thoughts were like bloodless shadows of conscience and logic" (p. 136). It is only natural that the Earth should prefer an artist so susceptible to the beauties of her landscapes, to an intellectual like Smith who seems so ethereal in his search for Platonic realities. Harriet will discover later that there's more to Smith than that, but for the moment he does indeed seem more like Shelley than Shaw.

Smith's diffident search for identity naturally takes him into the society of art and philosophy to discover what sort of Artist-Philosopher he is to be.[45] Once again he does not seem to care for contemporary models. Cyril Scott is among the less fraudulent members of Perspective society, yet even he has serious flaws of personality. The character of Scott is perhaps an indication of what Shaw, or any other artist, might become if he allowed his sensibility to dominate his personality. (Incidentally, Shaw reveals in the preface, p. xliii, that as a boy he always "wanted to be a painter, never a writer.") Scott is a monster of artistic pride, never relaxing for a minute his scorn of critics, amateurs, and mediocrity. "There were scarcely four artists in England whom Scott liked, and not more than two who liked him" (p. 131). Although he is not without some affectation in dress and manner, and is "superficially spoiled," it is clear that Scott is a genuine craftsman and a superior artist among the assorted frauds of Perspective. He could look "at the setting sun with a workmanlike attention which contrasted with the gloomy absorption affected by some others present" (p. 117). Scott is hampered in the war of art theories by being "so in earnest that his own irony, labored and sometimes coarse, seemed less a weapon than a wound" (p. 131). He has developed a reputation for being a rather blunt, uncordial sort whose esthetic honesty will counte-

45. The connection between Smith and the people at Perspective is made when we discover that after leaving Islington Smith took up residence on Danvers Street because it was near Cheyne Walk, the name of which "was suggestive to Smith of poets, artists, philosophers, picturesque old houses, blue and white china, wooden bridges, floating piers, and penny steamers" (p. 88). Incidentally, Cheyne Walk, Chelsea, was the residence of the Malcolm Lawsons, very nearly the only friends Shaw had in those early London years. Shaw relates how he often stood outside their house, suffering agonies of shyness, before getting up nerve to knock. See Henderson, p. 132.

nance no flattery, either to or from himself. Although he is beginning to win a reluctant recognition, Scott feels no gratitude after experiencing so many bitter disappointments. In short, he is Neglected Genius personified, the personification of a well-nourished feeling within the being of the obscure young Shaw. The problem for any young, unknown artist is to keep that feeling from distorting one's personality. The young Shaw, for instance, writes of Smith that it was good for him that he "received no encouragement to indulge in that clamor for sympathy, the whining expression of which is sometimes regarded . . . as a sort of trade mark of genius" (p. 83). The sort of artist who trades on his sensibility soon becomes nothing but sensibility, or rather nothing but the appearance of sensibility.

That is why Shaw engages Cyril Scott in an amorous debate with Harriet Russell. Debate is needed to clarify for the reader the issue of sense and sensibility, as it pertains to the identification of Smith. The debate between sense and sensibility in the persons of Harriet and Scott is an objectification of a debate taking place within the psyche of Smith.

Round one of this debate occurs in a Perspective gallery, where Scott accidentally meets Harriet as she is viewing one of his impressionistic paintings, "Fretted with Golden Fires." After much agonizing protocol, Harriet is induced to criticize his painting, unaware that it is his. Unfortunately for the painter she has "her thimble on," meaning that the practical dressmaker can see only affectation in the painting, "as if the painter was thinking a good deal about himself" (p. 134). She is further dismayed to learn that Grosvenor paid four hundred and fifty pounds for it, concluding that it must have been out of pity for the artist. Scott is momentarily floored by all this, but eventually comes to see the truth of it. In the course of his affair with Harriet, he learns the lesson of his prideful and querulous nature.

In the debate between sense and sensibility it is clear that sense has all the advantage, for it is part of sense's character never to make a fool of herself. Sensibility, on the other hand, never fails to make a fool of himself. This is symbolically conveyed in a comic scene upon the river involving Scott, Harriet, and Hawkshaw. Harriet expertly does the sculling of the boat until Hawkshaw's gallantry and Scott's humiliation force her to hand over the oars. Although the two artists had been expert enough at appreciating the idyllic scenes they had been rowed through, they are miserable failures at pulling the oars of common industry. They clumsily smite themselves with the oars and nearly capsize the boat, saved only by Harriet's quick agility. As the two artists nurse their wounded sensibilities, Harriet rows the boat to shore with an extra pair of sculls.

While Hawkshaw good-naturedly luxuriates in his humiliation, Scott remains stiff-necked and pettish. Harriet points out the difference to Scott, who defends himself with a long speech on the trials and tribulations of being an artist. The special strains of artistic creation, he argues, make "the gratuitous worries of commonplace life doubly unendurable. Just think of all this when you see me irritated for a moment by some trifle; and above all, remember that it is this very sensitiveness which makes sympathy so indescribably precious to an artist" (p. 285). Harriet replies that this need for sympathy is "nothing but a fashion. . . . People nowadays are proud of being pettish, and think it a great thing to say that they are hard to please; that they cant bear this, and cant endure that; that they are misunderstood" (p. 286). Scott indignantly wants to know if she thinks "an artist's feelings are as blunt as those of a stockbroker." Harriet defends her class, and adds a Shavian moral: "I dont see why a stockbroker should not have feelings like an artist; although he has to learn to keep them to himself, and to know his place in the world. But in any case, if an artist is superior in feeling, he ought to be just as superior in self-control."[46] It is interesting that many of Harriet's opinions on art and artists are quotations of Smith. He has taught her that the artist who does not know that his displays of temperament are only theatrically amusing is a great fool, and this lesson she teaches to Scott. The influence of Smith begins to spread.

46. Shaw later insisted that the Superman would be known by his self-control, rather than by his control over others or nature. See my article, "Shaw and the Passionate Mind," *The Shaw Review,* pp. 2–11.

Robert Hogan raises the question of the consistency of Shaw's characterizations. Hogan believes that there is some "wavering of line" in the drawing of Smith, Scott, and Harriet.[47] Why, for instance, did Shaw make Scott part artistic poseur and part genuine artist? Why, in short, didn't he make Scott 100 per cent poseur like Hawkshaw? The answer is the obvious one that Shaw wanted to distinguish between two different kinds or gradations of artistic immaturity for the sake of more clearly defining the character of Smith. Scott's posing is the result of an aggravated pride and sensibility, behind which there is real talent, whereas the posing of Hawkshaw is the result of an incorrigible, if entertaining, dishonesty. Scott is earnest where Hawkshaw is gaily deceiving. Scott plays the role of artist in order to defend himself against doubts of his talent, whereas Hawkshaw assumes the disguise of artist purely for the delight of impersonation. The point of the distinction is that Robert Smith avoids both sorts of impersonation, for they are merely clichés acceptable to society which do nothing more than warp the personality of the true artist to the point where he is more concerned with looking like an artist than actually being an artist. Cyril Scott comes to see (as the result of a lesson passed along from Smith to Harriet) that he can stand alone on the product of his genius and need not squeeze himself into anyone's image of what an artist should be. Shaw never tired of exemplifying the point that people are what people do, not what they look to be. A true artist is someone who creates true art, and nothing else.

The character of Harriet Russell too is more consistent than seems the case. To Hogan, Harriet seems to transform suddenly from the "merely unlearned, drably matter-of-fact, and quietly opinionated" young dressmaker of the first book to the straight-talking, clear-sighted, rationalistic, unconventional New Woman of the rest of the novel. Shaw started out to draw a Philistine, thinks Hogan, and wound up drawing "the Shavian New Woman à la Vivie Warren."[48] While I agree that the Harriet of the final three books is somewhat different from the Harriet

47. Hogan, p. 70.
48. *Ibid.*

of the first book, I do not agree that that difference constitutes an inconsistency in characterization. For one thing, Harriet Russell takes a while to get to know. On first acquaintance, she seems a rather different person from what she becomes after a certain degree of intimacy. Hawkshaw, for instance, had at first thought her "made of steel, with a heart of snow, triply Scotch, the idealization of matter-of-fact, the sepulchre of emotion, the shrine and sanctuary of canniness" (p. 257). To the poet she was a desert, in which the fertile sensibilities of poor Cyril would wither and die. But after the boating incident, Hawkshaw recants: "She is altogether charming. When I said she had no softness, no feeling, no sympathy, I blasphemed. Beneath the veil of her incomparable originality, she is made up of all three" (p. 287). Thus rather than Harriet's character undergoing a change in this respect, it is more a matter of the reader changing his opinion about her because he knows her better.

For another thing, if Harriet seems to transform from the Philistine female to the "New Woman à la Vivie Warren," as Hogan supposes, it is due largely to a change of company. Who among us remains always the same whatever the company he keeps? Shaw right from the beginning seemed to understand a subtle point of characterization—namely, that personality is relative to environment.[49] What we are is often in response to where we are and with whom we are. It is quite natural that Harriet in the company of the "pale scholar of Islington" would be different from Harriet in the company of such poseurs as Hawkshaw and Cyril Scott. Harriet seems somewhat baffled and intimidated by the extraordinary Smith, whereas she is thoroughly competent to penetrate the foolish and transparent disguises of Scott and Hawkshaw.[50] Smith's hyper-rationalism and hyper-unconventionality make her own common sense and hereditary unconventionality seem pale by comparison, but when that

49. This is not true of the comedy of humors, of course. But Harriet is not a Jonsonian caricature, nor is *Immaturity* a comedy of humors.

50. Insofar as Smith himself is a poseur (he sometimes poses as the Shelleyan Radical), Harriet is able to debunk him quite as thoroughly as she does the others.

same common sense and unconventionality are put in contrast with the affected sensibilities and rigid proprieties of the Perspective crowd they do indeed make her look more like Smith than like the Philistine she really is. (Shaw never tired either of making the point that some Philistines, especially those unconventionally raised, are easily mistaken for Shavian "realists.") It is true that Harriet becomes more sure of herself after her marriage to Scott and her acceptance by society, that she is better educated (mostly by Smith) in her opinions on life and art, that she is less prissily girlish and more womanly-matronly, and that, in short, she is wiser for her experiences, but all of these changes are the natural result of experiences recounted in the novel. She is indeed a subtly developing and changing character, but she is not "suddenly transformed" from one sort of person to an entirely different sort. Beneath all the changes is a basic Philistinism that does not change, the ultimate proof of which is that she finds marriage perfectly comfortable, quite unlike Vivie Warren.

Hogan believes that Harriet and Smith provide two different standards of maturity, both unconventional, against which the immaturity of the other characters is gauged.[51] Harriet is a "rationalist" and Smith an austere "super-rationalist," thus making the other characters seem immature in their various kinds of emotionalism. However, Hogan also believes that they both arrive at their separate kinds of maturity by paths not clearly shown in the novel. Shaw, says Hogan, "does not show Smith so much in the process of a believable change as he merely reveals a different Smith in different stages of the novel."[52] Once again I think Hogan has not looked closely enough at the detail of the characterization, nor has he allowed sufficiently for the possibility of different environments bringing out different facets of personality. The fact is that Smith is essentially the same throughout the novel, and everything he does later in the novel is adequately prepared for in the early characterization. Smith's quiet flirtation with Harriet in the opening book foreshadows the later, more boisterous flirtation with Isabella. If Smith in the

51. Hogan, p. 70.
52. *Ibid.*, p. 72.

latter flirtation seems unlike Smith in the former, that is simply because Isabella, the professional flirt, is quite unlike the more serious Harriet, who has no time for such silly games. If Smith seems more comic in the scenes with the Woodwards than with Harriet, that is because the Woodwards are more comic themselves and thus bring out the comic potential in Smith. If in the scenes with Harriet in the epilogue Smith seems wiser than at the beginning, that wisdom is less his own than a reflection of the relative maturity achieved by Harriet. Had the novel closed with a scene involving Smith with Mrs. Froster, Smith doubtless would have seemed as jejune as always. Actually, Smith is not much further along in his quest for a positive identity at the end than at the beginning.

In the conversation that closes the novel, Harriet remarks that she doesn't think Smith was "ever really a boy at all." Smith agrees that he "never felt like one." Harriet replies, "That is the puzzle about you. You are not a boy; and you are not grown-up. Some day you will get away from your books and come to know the world and get properly set. But just now there is no doing anything with you. You are just a bad case of immaturity" (p. 423). Hogan is right, I believe, in declaring Harriet one standard of maturity, her maturity being nothing more than an unusual Philistine commonsense maturity, but he is surely mistaken in his assumption that Smith is "not immature, merely inexperienced."[53] Inexperience is certainly the case, but more fundamental to Smith is the awkward immaturity of most of his responses to the life he sees around him. Undoubtedly Smith seems mature in comparison with many of the other characters, but most of them are so childish that that does not say much for Smith. A major point of the novel is that Smith, immaturely, does not know where he is going. He merely drifts. Whatever identity he achieves is purely negative. He knows that he is *not* Fraser Fenwick, he is *not* St. John Davis, he is *not* Cyril Scott, he is *not* Hawkshaw, and so forth, but he does not know who Robert Smith *is*. That, incidentally, accounts for the backward push of the novel. Its principal action consists of saying no. Granted that

53. *Ibid.*, p. 72.

a novel with a forward thrust is more satisfying to read because of a natural inclination on the part of the reader for positive movement, but of course the type of hero the reader prefers to identify with has absolutely nothing to do with the novel's performance of art. A novel with a forward thrust is not, by definition, superior to a novel with a negative movement.

In the final action of the novel, Smith departs from Harriet with the verdict of his immaturity, and after stopping to contemplate the contrasting patches of moonlight and black shadow beneath a Thames bridge, he "at last . . . shook his head negatively, and went home" (p. 424). That tiny shake of the head is a vastly summarizing action that at once dismisses the life into which he has been accidentally cast and points to the nature of his immaturity. In dismissing the black and white categories of his age (objectified perhaps in the patches of moonlight and black shadow), he finds himself still in quest of a "home," a permanent center of authority, as opposed to the temporary lodgings of Islington and Danvers Street. In short, the shake of the head signals Smith's plunge into a moral and religious vacuum.[54]

That the literary descendants of Smith will find a way out of that vacuum is perhaps indicated by certain rather curious opinions of Smith on the subject of belief. At one point Smith says, "Every man who entertains a belief, or a disbelief, has a right to become a propagandist, both for the sake of testing himself and enlightening others" (p. 414). This seems out of character for the diffident Smith, but it can be made to fit the character of the young rationalist if we understand that it is presented as a tentative proposition, far from being practiced by Smith himself. More difficult to fit into the character of Smith is the following: "There is no real difference [between bigotry and religion]. . . .

54. About that vacuum, Eric Bentley wrote, "The freedom of the tepidly Christian home made it easy for Shaw to proceed to the second state of Victorian belief: belief in unbelief, faith in the liberating power of a No-God. For when religion is mainly negative, the rejection of religion seems mainly positive, and men can be enthusiastic about a vacuum. . . . The earliest novels, insofar as they breathe anything, breathe the agnostic atmosphere." *Bernard Shaw, 1856–1950*, p. 45.

The only man in The Pilgrim's Progress who is not a bigot is Mr
Worldly Wiseman. I would not give a halfpenny for the faith
of a votary who would not cut off the whole human race if it
differed from him" (p. 269). This sounds like the mature, evangelistic Shaw all right, the Shaw much given to overstatement,
but does it fit the character of Smith? Is it consistent with his
rationalistic approach to advocate anything beyond reasonable
argumentation in behalf of a belief or disbelief? It would not
seem so, unless we have misunderstood the character of Smith.
Perhaps the justification is that in drawing Smith, Shaw intended
to portray not merely a rationalist; rather he meant to present
a young man who, immaturely, only *thinks* he is a rationalist,
a young man who is prevented from becoming a thundering
prophet by a critical intelligence and a natural diffidence that
combine to stifle his many natural impulses to evangelize. Deep
in that chivalric soul of his Smith is a natural champion of the
Faith. The trouble is that he's not quite sure what that Faith is,
although he knows what it is not. It is not anything presently
organized, that's for sure. Like himself, his Faith still needs to be
defined. If we misunderstand Smith's character, it is because
Smith himself misunderstands it.

Thus the general charge that Shaw was inconsistent in his
characterizations is not, in most cases, well founded. Even less
viable is the complaint, typical to almost all of Shaw's work, that
Immaturity is inartistically "talky" and propagandistic. Because
of Shaw's preoccupation with ideas, he is thought to be inartistic
in his neglect of the traditional forms of their expression—that
is, in character and action. Henderson, for instance, accuses
Shaw of being "interested in fiction, not on the score of literary
technique, but as a medium for the expression of ideas."[55] Shaw
did not agree with this, and obviously neither do I. Shaw said
that, "as to the literary execution of the books, I suppose it will
not now be questioned that I am no mere man of genius, but a
conscientious workman as well."[56] *Of course* Shaw was inter-

55. Henderson, p. 95.
56. "Mr. Bernard Shaw's Works of Fiction Reviewed by Himself,"
Novel Review, p. 243.

ested in expressing ideas, and *of course* his novels are for that reason talky, but surely the desire to express ideas through dialogue does not preclude art.

For one thing, talkiness in itself can be a trait of character. For another, if one wishes to portray a rather sedate society that is more noted for its talk than for its non-verbal actions, then obviously one's characters will be talky. Indeed, if one wishes to portray the teacup society of respectable Victorian England, then the chief action will be talk. Perhaps in primitive, heroic societies the heart and soul of the society is in its non-verbal actions, but in the drawing rooms of London the prime action is that of talk, and no novel that presumes to portray it can succeed without focusing upon its talk. If the chief action of Shaw's characters is talk, then that in itself is the most significant point about them. Now one may legitimately dislike talky novels, but one should not confuse that dislike with objective judgments upon the novels' art. It is quite possible to dislike a novel that is accurate in its portrayal, significant in its theme, and excellent in its art.

As for the charge that Shaw substituted propaganda for art, I have already shown that this novel is not very susceptible to that charge. I have shown how many of the characters and incidents which seem to have no function other than to carry Shavian arguments are really integral to the art of the novel. On this score, nothing can be more convincing than the fact that Smith himself is treated ironically by Shaw.[57] If Shaw were interested only in propagandizing Shelleyan ideas, he most certainly would not have made his spokesman look foolish and immature in the expression of those ideas. There are indeed times when Harriet and Smith and James Vesey,[58] an artist consulted by Scott on the subject of marriage, seem to speak directly for

57. The writing of *Immaturity* must have been tremendously therapeutic for Shaw, as it meant that he was able to encompass, to contain in art, and thus to control his former immaturity.

58. I agree with Hogan that Vesey and Grosvenor are rather unfinished characters. They are so impressively introduced that one expects to see a great deal more of them.

Shaw, but whenever they do their talk is always an agent of plot, theme, and characterization.

There is no point in defending the novel in every line, however. Two scenes are especially questionable. One night Smith returns to his room in Danvers Street to find his landlady, Mrs. Tilly, being addressed over the head with a saucepan by her drunken husband. This scene of domestic violence challenges Smith's natural diffidence until he can bear it no longer and comes to the rescue of the "damsel." He gets no thanks for it at the time, as Mrs. Tilly believes that in submitting to such a beating she was only doing her conjugal duty, but the next day she apologizes to Smith and laments the influence of spirits upon her normally gentle and loving husband. " 'I wouldnt mind so much,' said Mrs. Tilly with a stifled sob, 'only for the child. I wish the government would shut up them wicked public houses, and keep honest men that would never unhappify their homes without them, from temptation' " (pp. 168–69). Now that speech may be perfectly in character, and it may indirectly contribute to the theme of immaturity, but it sounds suspiciously like prohibition propaganda.

In another scene, the propaganda is blatant. During Smith's visit to a cemetery Shaw has him overhear a conversation between a gentleman and a gravedigger, in which the gravedigger holds forth on the evils of coffin burial. It seems the coffin will explode unless the digger drills a hole in them to let out the gas from the corrupted corpse, and the gas has been known to kill a man. After this scene Shaw years later appended an unfortunate footnote which reads: "In 1878 this scene was something more than a description of the macabre side of a young man's fancy. It was a plea for cremation, which was then a much more controversial subject than it is now. And it was a repleading of Dickens's protest against the grotesque mummeries of the old-fashioned funerals" (p. 172). So Shaw convicts himself out of his own mouth. It is noteworthy that the two scenes described here immediately follow one another in the novel, and in this same chapter is Smith's departure from the capitalistic firm of Figgis & Weaver. Granted that all three scenes are more or less worked into the general development of character and theme, I nevertheless believe that Shaw was momentarily feeling more like a social reformer than an artist when he wrote them. They make the chapter in question come as close to being inartistic as any chapter in any of Shaw's novels.

The charge that *Immaturity* is often irrelevant in its detail (and irrelevant usually because propagandistic) is one that cannot be completely refuted in anything less than another two hundred pages, as it would require a defense of every single detail. Obviously I can do no better here, in the little space I have, than provide a representative sample. For my purposes the more minor and insignificant the detail seems, the better a demonstration of its relevance will convince skeptical critics of the relevance of more important details. I choose the following scene not only because it seems insignificant, but also because it presumably demonstrates what Irvine calls Shaw's "clerkish conscientiousness."[59] In this scene Smith is described in the Islington lodging house unpacking his things. He had some hand-knitted socks, but "other underclothing he had none." His parents "had been too poor and too careless to make him any fixed allowance," and his wages as a clerk are little more than subsistence. Among his treasures were a family Bible, a Shakespeare, and the works of Byron. In an old tool chest he kept two toy brass cannons and some chemistry equipment, sad "relics of his boyhood, and proofs of his homelessness; for who ever removes such things from his father's house whilst any of his kin are to be found there?" Evidences of an unusual culture were a few sheets of music and a Dürer drawing "representing a knight accompanied by Death and followed by a demon, both of them grotesquely goatish" (pp. 5-6). That this itemizing of Smith's belongings occurs in the novel for no other reason than that Shaw had not yet rid himself of the bookkeeping mentality of his former Dublin clerkship is extremely unlikely. A critic would have to be exceedingly desperate in his eagerness to debunk and ridicule in order to say anything quite as silly as that. For obviously Smith's belongings are

59. Irvine, p. 24. The actual scene Irvine refers to is that of Mrs. Froster's drawing room, the description of which I have already defended.

minutely described by Shaw to make the point that they are few
in number, that Smith, still carrying around "relics of his boyhood," is pathetically and prematurely alone, and that Smith,
an unusually cultured young man, carries about with him the
Dürer drawing as an image of his own menaced, chivalric figure.
And so it is with the rest of the novel. I find evidence on every
page that Shaw knew exactly what he was doing and why he
was doing it.

On the question of the formality of *Immaturity*'s language,
however, I am not perfectly certain that Shaw was conscious of
the fitness of that language. *Immaturity* is the most stiff and conventionally rhetorical of Shaw's novels, a fact that one would
ordinarily attribute to an unsuccessful attempt to escape the
formal language patterns of contemporary fiction. Shaw later
abandoned this style and, along with all the critics, condemned
it as "unnatural." But what about the critical ideal which calls
for a harmony of language and character? What if you are writing a novel about a young Victorian who is rather stiff and
unnatural in his behavior? Would not such a young man be best
represented by a style which was also stiff and unnatural? The
style fits the man, and surely a more natural style would not have
succeeded as well in capturing the unnaturalness of the novel's
hero. If Smith, for instance, were to speak in the more modern
tongue of Edward Conolly, the hero of Shaw's second novel, he
would have been considerably less like Smith. I am forced to conclude that in imitating the fashionable language of the day's fiction, Shaw wrote better than he knew, for the point about Smith
is that he is so unsure of himself that, for the sake of seeming
correct, he imitates the language that is fashionably correct. I
cannot imagine Smith speaking any other way without ceasing
to be Smith.

I hope I have not given the impression that Shaw, prior to
Hogan, was totally alone in his secret regard for the art of his
nonage. Several reputable critics have been extravagant in their
praise of Shaw as novelist. James Huneker somewhat ambiguously opined that "for no one of his many gifts will he be so
sternly taken to task as the wasted one of novelist. . . . Shaw

could rank higher as a novelist than as a dramatist."[60] In view of Shaw's high ranking as a dramatist, that is wonderful praise indeed. Another of Shaw's American admirers, Christopher Morley, praises the novels to the disparagement of the plays.

> Well, the Daemon of the Epoch did have its effect on G.B.S. Whether for good or ill, it is too early to say. With his industry (as great as Trollope's), his seriousness (as intense as John Stuart Mill's), and his mad humor (as fierce as Meredith's), he might as well—and if publishers had had half an eye, certainly would—have gone on in a series of novels that would have been unlike anything in the course of British fiction. No one can read "The Man of Destiny," for instance, without saying, What a short story gone astray! No one can read "Cashel Byron's Profession" . . . without seeing its extraordinary charm, humour and spoofing. . . . I myself regard him as a great novelist gone wrong.[61]

As late as 1930 an anonymous critic for the *New Statesman* judged of Shaw's first novel that "if *Immaturity* had been published in 1880, it is certain that the novels of Gissing and Mark Rutherford would have been richer, more confident, than it was their fate to be. . . . There are signs in *Immaturity,* as also in *Love Among the Artists,* that Shaw might, had he chosen, have taken that place in the English novel which has been unfilled since the death of Thackeray."[62]

Huneker, Morley, and the anonymous critic may be right that Shaw was perfectly suited for the novel, but the novels ambiguously suggest the opposite as well, that Shaw became increasingly uninterested in the novel the more he wrote. There seems to be a disintegration, rather than a development, in Shaw's novel form in that the novels become more and more like prose dramas with long soliloquies, and they show less and less concern with meeting

60. James Huneker, "Bernard Shaw and Women," *Harper's Bazaar,* p. 536.

61. Quoted in Henderson, p. 129.

62. *Ibid.,* p. 112.

conventional standards of art. Only the first two novels are "finished," in the sense of having rounded-off conclusions. The third and fifth novels seem to have been cut off by an impatient author before they had been properly concluded, and the fourth novel so neatly conforms to a Victorian plot cliché that the use of it seems no more than a spoof.

One can think of many reasons for this increasing disregard for the novel. Perhaps the form of the novel was not particularly suited to Shaw's talents. Supposedly, the necessity for narration and prose exposition would conflict with Shaw's love of the purely dramatic. When Shaw writes prose, the argument goes, he writes like an essayist, a polemicist. Only when he embodies his ideas in the direct action of drama does he escape being a polemicist. In the drama his characters may lecture the audience, but not Shaw himself. There may be something to this argument but, first of all, I do not find Shaw seriously inept in the handling of narrative in his novels, and, secondly, I note that Shaw's plays have more prose exposition in the form of stage directions than those of any other playwright.[63] His need and his ability to use prose fictionally seems not to have diminished after he became a dramatist.

Others believe that Shaw abandoned the novel because, after becoming disenchanted with its conventions, he had failed to develop an effective and significantly different novel form of his own. This argument has more merit, but there are signs in at least three of his novels that he was moving in a positive direction toward something distinctly Shavian in the way of a novel. Shaw's disintegration as a novelist can be attributed to the need to destroy Victorian conventions before he could build upon his own foundations. Perhaps as the Victorian novel disintegrates in Shaw's hands, something else is being erected to replace it. If we can accept the "dialogue novel" or the "novel of ideas" as legitimate developments, then we can better credit Shaw with a sig

63. For a review of critics who think Shaw wrote novels like a dramatist, or dramas like a novelist, see Stanley Weintraub's "The Embryo Playwright in Bernard Shaw's Early Novels," *The University of Texas Studies in Literature and Languages,* pp. 327–29.

nificant contribution to the development of the novel. At any rate, that Shaw drifted further and further from the conventional Victorian novel form is a certainty; whether that argues a plunge into an esthetic vacuum or the development of a new base for the novel is very uncertain.

More certainly Shaw's steadily falling interest in the novel was due to increasing preoccupation with socialism and his role as a social reformer. Doubtless he must have wondered if he couldn't do something more effective to change the existing social order than write unpublished novels. Most convincing of all is the simple explanation that he grew tired of writing novels that no one would publish. How many people can be named who have continued to write novels after the first five have been refused by nearly every publishing house in England and America? The fact that Shaw did write five novels before giving up (and started a sixth a few years later) is one of the most astonishing things about him.

Whether for any or all of the above reasons, from *Immaturity* on it is mostly downhill for the young Shaw as far as the art of the novel is concerned. At the age of twenty-three he sat down to write something as much like a novel as he could make it. He was really sincere about writing a *novel,* as his contemporaries would have understood the word. He was fairly pious, as pious as Shaw ever could be, about the conventions of the Victorian novel. But the more he wrote, the less pious he became and the more destructive he became in regard to those conventions. Therefore I believe that *Immaturity* is Shaw's best novel, not only because it contains his most memorable and significant char- acter, but because in it he tries to do less on his own and is more at peace with conventional techniques. The other novels (with the exception of *Cashel Byron's Profession,* a special case) ambi- tiously attempt a reformation of the novel, and therefore succeed less well, torn as they are between the destruction of the old and construction of the new. The perfectly astounding truth is that at the age of twenty-three Shaw had virtually mastered the con- ventions and artifices of the English novel. In subsequent novels he became increasingly uninterested in those conventions and artifices and increasingly fascinated by the character of the hero.

Hogan writes that "one will never understand Shaw's five novels by assuming that Shaw really condemned them, that his remarks were accurate, or that the novels themselves are jejune work." Quite the contrary, says Hogan, "if we scrutinize the novels clearly, we will find much more than jejune work; indeed, I think that we will find the charge of immaturity can only be made by a narrow taste or an imperceptive reading, as impervious to subtlety as it is insensitive to wit and ignorant of delight."[64] While the title of Shaw's first novel certainly does apply to Robert Smith, it does not apply to the twenty-three-year-old author who created him. There is hardly a page of this novel in which the young novelist does not display an understanding or technique that argues a maturity well beyond his years. It would be just as impossible for a truly immature Shaw to have written *Immaturity* as for a truly innocent Blake to have written *Songs of Innocence,* for as surely as innocence knows not itself, the truly immature is unaware of its immaturity. Shaw's measure to the nearest fraction of the immaturity of both society and his teen-age hero suggests the insights and skill of a man nearer forty than twenty-three. The proof of this contention is in the sudden maturity of the hero of Shaw's second novel.

64. Hogan, p. 65.

Life and Art

The best autobiographies are confessions; but if a man is a deep writer all his works are confessions.

BERNARD SHAW
Sixteen Self-Sketches

I have no clue to any historical or other personage save that part of him which is also myself. . . . The man who writes about himself and his own time is the only man who writes about all people and about all time.

BERNARD SHAW
The Sanity of Art

Unless we are replaced by . . . the Superman—the world must remain a den of dangerous animals among whom our few accidental supermen, our Shakespeares, Goethes, Shelleys, and their like, must live as precariously as lion tamers do, taking the humor of their situation, and the dignity of their superiority, as a set-off to the horror of the one and the loneliness of the other.

JOHN TANNER
"The Revolutionist's Handbook"

The only fundamental and possible Socialism is the socialization of the selective breeding of Man: in other terms, of human evolution. We must eliminate the Yahoo, or his vote will wreck the commonwealth.

JOHN TANNER
"The Revolutionist's Handbook"

The Novels as Autobiography

Readers of Shaw's novels may come to them for a variety of reasons. Perhaps the mere fact that Shaw is a major author will attract some. My first reading of *Immaturity* occurred for no better reason. Others knowing that they have been gloriously entertained in the plays and prefaces may come to the novels for more of the same. If so, they will not be disappointed, for Shaw found it difficult to be dull, even when he tried. Still others who will not bother with anything they suspect to be inept may have been convinced that the novels are worth reading because artfully written. In the preceding essay I have tried to show that the novels are both entertaining and skillfully written, work indeed worthy of a major author. But the rest of this study is aimed at those who would read the novels because they are fascinated by the man himself. To them I hold out the promise of discovering in Shaw's novels something about their author that cannot be found anywhere else.

While Shaw himself thought highly enough of his novels to promote their publication, it is clear that his promotion of them was not based entirely upon his conviction of their artistic worth. Rather he had other reasons for wanting the public to see them. At the age of ninety-one Shaw wrote, "My imagination has always rearranged facts into stories."[1] The "always" was only a small exaggeration, for biographies of his boyhood reveal an excessively imaginative child whose romancing seems to have begun soon after birth. There is no reason to suppose that in writing his novels he temporarily abandoned his habit of placing himself in a fictional environment and took up instead the naturalistic method of objective reporting. "All my happenings," Shaw said, "have taken the form of books and plays."[2] He believed that "the best autobiographies are confessions; but if a man is a

1. Henderson, p. 946.
2. Bernard Shaw, *Sixteen Self-Sketches*, p. 6.

deep writer all his works are confessions."[3] Given such explicit statements of Shaw's inveterate habit of dramatizing and fiction-alizing his thought and experience, the critic is certainly justified in reading Shaw's art as an autobiography of the artist's mind. I will further maintain that the novels constitute an autobiography that their author very much wanted people to read for the purely personal reason of making them more friendly (because more understanding) toward himself.

The novels thus hold an importance out of proportion to whatever value they have as art due to their initial position in the Shavian line of development; they show us how Bernard Shaw experimentally created the person he became, how he molded the soft clay of immaturity into the man and superman that everyone took for granted in the later Shaw. What is being developed in these novels is not so much the art of the novel as the art of being Bernard Shaw. The novels describe an artistic process that will certainly fascinate and perhaps astonish anyone who through reading Shaw's plays and prefaces has come to believe that Shaw was always Shaw. He may very well have possessed a degree of his own Caesar's "magical invulnerability," but the novels suggest rather that the issue was often in doubt, that the young Shaw was constantly on the brink of becoming some other person, a person we might have liked considerably less well than we liked the person he did become. All this the plays tell us nothing about, for the first play did not "hit the boards" until 1892 when Shaw was thirty-six, a fully mature adult, if not a fully mature dramatist. The novels, on the other hand, were written from 1879 to 1883, from the ages of twenty-three to twenty-seven, the crucial years for the shaping of Shaw's life and art. They are, therefore, indispensable guides to the character of their author in that they reveal, as the plays do not, the experimental piecing together of the unique Shavian person-ality and world view. The plays show rather the struggle to maintain or adapt to changing circumstances an identity long established.

The great importance and fascination of these novels, then,

3. *Ibid.*

is not so much in their display of literary art, though that is respectable enough, as in their display of the art of personality. Shaw has said that "no person is real until he has been transmuted into a work of art."[4] The primary value of Shaw's novels is that they preserve the record of his own marvelous transmutation. They remind us too of the extreme importance of art for life's sake.

4. Stephen Winsten, *Days with Bernard Shaw*, p. 187.

The Proper Study of Mankind Is Superman

This study of Shaw is not just to draw a "portrait of the artist," but rather a "portrait of the artist *as a young superman*." The word "superman" extremely complicates the task of reading the novels as autobiography, for it suggests that their portrayal is not of the ordinary man but of the extraordinary man, not of Bernard Shaw as he usually was but as he often wanted to be and perhaps occasionally was.[1] Yet, what a man wants to be is very much a part of what he is—perhaps the core of a man. Our longings for the divine, especially as manifested in our visions of the super-human, are most us, for they best reveal the quality of our human-ity. As Caliban is best characterized by his view of the super-human, so too with Mohammed, St. Paul, and the like. It follows then that what Bernard Shaw was like as a man is most clearly revealed in his aspirations toward the superhuman. That he aspired to be a Superman is obvious, but what precisely is a Superman? A thorough and convincing answer can only be arrived at inductively, after a careful analysis of those works which, I maintain, infer a definition, but for the sake of orienta-tion I include here a tentative theory of the Superman, to be tested later against the reality of the novels.

The later plays and prefaces help a good deal in piecing to-gether a theory of the Superman. It is clear why the Superman is necessary. According to John Tanner in "The Revolutionist's Handbook,"[2] man as he is presently constituted is incapable of

1. Customarily Shaw capitalized "Superman" when he referred to the total concept or the whole species or the special quality of life it repre-sents, and did not capitalize it when referring to individual supermen. I will follow the same system.

2. Of course John Tanner is not Bernard Shaw, and we must be care-ful not to assume a complete identity between them. Yet Tanner is a literary expression of a very important part of Shaw, at times the domi-nant part, and we must therefore give him his due. The whole Shaw

rising beyond a certain point of civilization, because the qualities which allowed him to found a "commercial civilization"—namely, pugnacity, fanaticism, and cupidity—are the same qualities which inevitably lead him to fall back to the level of the savagery from which he arose.[3] Further, although man can temporarily achieve commercial civilization, he simply does not possess the will nor the energy to climb to the vast heights of that Utopia he aspires to. And even if he could achieve Utopia, man as he is would not be happy there.

But if man as he is does not possess the will and energy to achieve Utopia, how then can he hope to will the Superman into being, the latter surely being a more difficult task? Shaw's answer seems to be that in willing the Superman man has Nature on his side, in that the world's will seems to be driving at ever higher forms of life, forms which would not seem to be within the capacities of the lower forms themselves. Who, looking at a chimpanzee (or whatever beast is supposed to be our direct ancestor), would expect a chimp to be capable of creating a man? Yet the thing has happened, according to the argument of Shaw's Creative Evolution, because the Life Force willed it and could manage it with or without the cooperation of the species being superseded.

The next question is the crucial one. If the Life Force can evolve without the cooperation of its life forms, what then does it matter if man wills the Superman or not? What does it matter if the Superman arises from the heights of man's aspiration or from the depths of his despair? If, historically, the condition of mankind is simply better or worse, will the better produce the Superman through the intensity of its effort and aspiration, or will the worse produce the Superman through the intensity of its revulsion and desperate longing? Shaw's answer here seems to be that as the Life Force has been rather blindly experimenting

---

would doubtless have many qualifications to make of Tanner's philosophy, especially its harsher aspects, but Tanner's main argument, I feel certain, is Shaw's too.

3. Bernard Shaw, "The Revolutionist's Handbook," *Man and Superman*, III, 709.

with various life forms in a generally upward trend over billions of years, it now has created in man a species capable of intelligent participation in the next step and will, further, actually benefit from that participation. Man will be replaced sooner or later by something else, but what that something else is, the quality of its life, can be better or worse according to the intelligence of the will that creates it. If the Life Force is left to muddle on as it has for eons, its next evolutionary effort may not be much more of an improvement over man than the dinosaur was over the amphibian. Indeed, if the world's best mind makes no contribution, there actually may be some loss involved in such an evolution, as there certainly was in the case of the dinosaur and the amphibian.

Of course the assumption behind all this is that this progression of life forms we call evolution is meaningful to the universe, and more, that economy of its resources is vitally important. In the Shavian ethic, waste of life is the greatest sin, for Shaw sensed in the Life Force an urge to progress in time as speedily as possible. The fact of evolution itself is not only important, but how fast it occurs and what forms it creates are also very crucial. With the prospect of atomic doom very real before us, we no longer wonder at Shaw's rather apocalyptic sense of urgency.

If it was crucial to Shaw in the first years of this century that the Life Force evolve the Superman, it seems even more important to us in the closing decades of this century that the quality of life be improved, else we stand an excellent chance of destroying ourselves.[4] As events push the great nations toward a confronta-

4. I note, with increased respect for Shaw's foresight, that in 1901 he had John Tanner express the following: "We may as well make up our minds that Man will return to his idols and his cupidities, in spite of all 'movements' and all revolutions, until his nature is changed. Until then, his early successes in building commercial civilizations (and such civilizations, Good Heavens!) are but preliminaries to the inevitable later stage, now threatening us, in which the passions which built the civilization become fatal instead of productive, just as the same qualities which make the lion king in the forest ensure his destruction when he enters a city. . . . War and competition, potent instruments of selection and evolution in

tion, the conviction grows on intelligent persons that we have engendered forces far beyond our ability to control. Our tech-nology has seemingly dwarfed us. What is needed is a race of giants, Supermen indeed. But what sort of person is the Super-man to be, and how is he to be created by mere man?

Bernard Shaw did his part as an artist to provide clear shapes for the imagination to seize upon. Certainly his Caesar is a vivid model, as well as his Saint Joan, and we could do far worse than to imitate them. But, though he provided excellent models, he resolutely, and perhaps wisely, refused to state the exact specifi-cations of the Superman, for, as John Tanner says, "the proof of the Superman will be in the living; and we shall find out how to produce him by the old method of trial and error, and not by waiting for a completely convincing prescription of his ingredi-ents."[5] That then is what great men like Napoleon and Caesar and Cromwell, to name a few, are all about. They are attempts by the Life Force to form the heroic, the superhuman. If such attempts are largely failures, and often disastrous failures at that, it is because "God Himself cannot raise a people above its own level."[6] History shows that isolated supermen cannot, "except for a short time and by morally suicidal coercive methods, impose superhumanity on those whom they govern."[7] What is needed is a "Democracy of Supermen."[8] Shaw's call for the Superman was not so much a call for individual heroes, though such are important for experimental purposes, but for a whole world of Supermen.

Is not such an ambition rather extravagant? Perhaps it is, but it seems less extravagant when we consider how ancient and reputable it is. For the idea of the Superman, as conceived by Shaw, is in the mainstream of that long tradition of humanism bequeathed to us by the ancient Greeks, a humanism, further-

one epoch, become ruinous instruments of degeneration in the next" ("The Revolutionist's Handbook," pp. 712–13).
 5. *Ibid.,* p. 692.
 6. *Ibid.,* p. 700.
 7. *Ibid.,* p. 704.
 8. *Ibid.,* p. 705.

more, often enough practiced to make us sanguine of continued, and perhaps increased, success. That is, to the objection that the Superman is a goal impossibly out of reach, one must reply that the Superman has already happened and is happening.

At first sight the words "humanism" and "Superman" would seem to be mutually exclusive, even antagonistic, for the Super-man has often been dismissed as "science-fiction," and non-humanistic science-fiction at that. After the Hitler debacle, we hardly see the Superman mentioned in criticism without scorn or condemnation. At best it is treated only as a silly, comic-book idea. A somewhat gentler scoffing tone has appeared in Shaw criticism as well. The Superman is treated, usually by omission, as not central to Shaw's thought, as if it were just a momentary aberration, to be classed with other Shavian idiosyncrasies such as eating vegetables or wearing special suits, or as evidence of the artistic, sedentary man's uncritical enthusiasm for his opposite, the strong man. Further disqualification of the Superman as a serious humanistic idea would seem to be found, in Shaw's own work, in the "impractical" otherworldliness of his *Back to Methuselah* Ancients who strive to escape flesh for a whirlpool of pure thought. In light of all this, it is indeed difficult to take the Superman as anything more than a joke.

The obvious way out of this is to declare a state of semantic confusion and try to clear things up by defining a few words like "Superman" and "humanism." Shaw himself obscures things right at the outset by rascally announcing in *The Quintessence of Ibsenism* that "I do not deal in definitions."[9] This attitude seems irresponsible, especially in view of the nefarious uses of propaganda these days, but Shaw was of course fooling us again as in his many works his chief purpose is to define words whose meanings have become stale or obscured by use.[10] As for the attitude, nothing can be said in defense of it except that Shaw as propagandist was unusually concerned that words should en-

9. *Major Critical Essays,* in *Standard Edition,* p. 30.
10. For example, *Saint Joan* defines sainthood, *Caesar and Cleopatra* defines the heroic, *Mrs. Warren's Profession* defines respectability and capitalism, and *Major Barbara* defines charity.

lighten rather than deceive. He was wise enough to know that the whole truth is unknown to man and would be incapable of verbal expression even if it were known, words being the finite things that they are. All that can be said is that when Shaw propagandized he believed what he was saying, and believed because the propaganda pointed in the direction of some truth. Propaganda as a deliberate lie was unused by Bernard Shaw. While there was always room for many points of view in the interpretation of facts, the facts themselves, as far as they could be determined and represented by words, were not to be erroneously reported. Rather, propaganda was a way of shaping truth, of giving it linguistic form and religious force. Propaganda was for that which *ought* to be propagated.

What ought to be propagated, according to Shaw, is the idea of the Superman. But what about those Ancients in *Back to Methuselah* who are trying to escape flesh altogether for a whirlpool of pure thought? Are they Supermen? Certainly there doesn't seem to be anything humanistic about them, any more than about certain ascetic, otherworldly saints. Obviously, if one is going to include these rather ethereal beings in the definition of the Superman, that definition will either have to be subjected to classification, or we must conclude that the Ancients represent a development beyond or an alternative to the Superman. I am inclined to the latter view, as the vast majority of Shaw's life and work points toward a Superman who is not much given to *contemptus mundi,* as are the Ancients. The Ancients can be accounted for, I think, by a statement of John Tanner's (written in 1901 when Shaw was still a forty-five-year-old, hard-working Fabian socialist): "All who achieve real distinction in life begin as revolutionists. The most distinguished persons become more revolutionary as they grow older, though they are commonly supposed to become more conservative owing to their loss of faith in conventional methods of reform."[11] On the eve of World War II, the time of the writing of *Back to Methuselah,* Shaw must have wondered if even the Superman could save the world. Certainly the goose-stepping variety in Germany did not seem

11. "The Revolutionist's Handbook," p. 689.

promising. In his exasperation, then, he must have extended his view of the superhuman beyond the Superman to the Ancients.

For the sake of further definition, I would like to distinguish the Ancients and the qualities they represent from the Superman by the term "Anti-Man." The constant tension in Shaw between his worldliness and his otherworldliness, his naturalism and his supernaturalism, I equate with the struggle between the Super-man and the Anti-Man, a struggle created, on the one hand, by his Utopian aspirations for humanity and his love of human detail, and, on the other hand, by his "longing for the divine," as expressed in the figures of the Ancients, and by the everyday pressures of reality bearing upon a man who lived so intensely in the closest details of fleshly existence. In the mixture of Shavian being, the desire for release must have been commensurate with the passion for involvement.

The semantic dilemma caused by my assertion that the Super-man is essentially a humanistic idea is somewhat relieved by the substitution of Anti-Man for the Ancients, for it makes clearer a distinction between two kinds of superhumanity, but we are still left to explain the term "Super" in the word "Superman." How can that which is Super (meaning over) man be considered humanistic? The difficulty can be gotten over by seeing that the term "man" in either Superman or Anti-Man would be better understood as meaning Yahoo. Thus Super-Yahoo and Anti-Yahoo are the two poles of humanism and otherworldliness in disguise (i.e., in more conventional word usage). In short, Shaw's Superman is not much more or much less than what the great humanists have always meant by Man, and what I call Shaw's Anti-Man is not much more or much less than what the great otherworldly saints have always meant by Spiritual Man.

Our confusion over words is illustrated in the following:

1. J. S. Collis writes: "The proper study of mankind is not man, but Superman."

2. Blake writes: "In trying to be more than Man, We become less."

3. Browning writes: "Man is not man, as yet."

4. Pope writes: "The proper study of mankind is Man."

The seeming contradictions of these statements can be cleared up if we substitute "Yahoo" and "Super-Yahoo" in the proper places. Translated:

1. Collis means: "The proper study of Yahoo-kind is not Yahoo, but Super-Yahoo."

2. Blake means: "In trying to be more than Super-Yahoo, We become Yahoo or worse."

3. Browning means: "Yahoo is not Super-Yahoo, as yet."

4. Pope means: "The proper study of Yahoo-kind is Super-Yahoo."

Browning's meaning can perhaps be further clarified by these words from William Saroyan: "When I speak of the human race I speak of the *concealed* human race, the *still* concealed human race, which is trying to come out from under, as it has been trying for a million years or more. Will it come out from under in the next thousand?"[12]

The emergence of the "still concealed human race" is of course the chief concern of humanism, its highest ideal, just as the emergence of the concealed humanity within Bernard Shaw was the first concern of that young man, the ideal that preoccupied him until he took up the larger matter of universal improvement.[13] Shaw designated this emerging humanity the Superman, and gradually defined it in terms of the emerging humanity he observed, or thought he observed, in himself and in others, especially in heroes of the past like Caesar, Napoleon, Saint Joan, etc. But we should not be put off by a mere name. He called it the "Superman" only to distinguish it from the "Yahoo" he saw all about him, which went by the false name of "man." If Yahoos are going to call themselves "men," then real men have no choice but to call themselves "Supermen."

12. William Saroyan, *Here Comes—There Goes—You Know Who,* p. 175.

13. By "ideal" I mean a temporary goal or standard, the point upon which one's effort is bent. Customarily Shaw used ideal to designate that instrument of deceit whereby men disguise the real. When Shaw attacked ideals, he meant by the word those pretty pictures lodged in men's minds that serve as substitutes for the real. When he referred to his own ideals, he meant his goals.

Blake's warning to would-be Supermen about becoming "less than man" is well taken, but the danger, so vividly realized in Greek tragedy, seems to be less with the Superman (who, after all, is only trying to achieve true humanity) than with that part of the human psyche I have called the Anti-Man. It seems that men no sooner realize their humanity than they become discontented and wish for the impossible. Indeed, the danger of becoming truly human is that it can lead one to despise all that is material in preference of a higher, spiritual life, as with the Ancients. On the other hand, the Anti-Man can also be the result of frustration, the inability to achieve humanity. In Shaw's case, the inability of mankind in general to achieve true humanity undoubtedly inspired his more radical conception of the Ancients. When a goal becomes impossibly out of reach, one dreams not of achieving it but of going beyond it, or around it. Whether the discontent is with the truly human or the Yahoo, in this desire to be more than truly human, i.e., more than Superman, or Super-Yahoo, we risk becoming monsters. This is where Shaw himself, with his considerable portion of saintly temperament, stood his greatest risk. His salvation of course was his laughter, the comedy which provided the classical balance to his personality, the comedy which made him not just another crucifiable fanatic, but the privileged "fool in Christ."[14]

To further clarify the distinction between the Superman and the Anti-Man, the Superman is very much a creature of the flesh, and is partly defined by the way he puts flesh to its best use, while the Anti-Man is distinguished by his hatred of matter (not to be confused with hatred of life), a hatred that is proportionate to his love of the spirit. The Anti-Man is anti-humanist in his belief that flesh is a corruption of the spirit. The Superman is humanist in his belief that flesh is the proper material for the forming arts of the spirit. In this quarrel between the warring dualism of the Anti-Man and the pacific monism of the Superman, they are agreed in Shaw on only one point—on the desire for more and greater life, although each would define that word differently.

14. See the chapter entitled "The Fool in Christ" in Eric Bentley's *Bernard Shaw*.

The Superman defines life as the preservation of the spirit's ability to form and reform itself in the eternal art of material living;
the Anti-Man defines life as the escape from natural forms into
regions of pure spirit (or "pure thought," as Shaw would have
it). In short, the Anti-Man is a philosophical extension of the
Superman that provided a psychological release for Shaw, not
at all a practical ideal, in the sense of being realizable in matter.
The Superman, on the other hand, is very much practical and
worth striving for with our merely human (Yahoo) energies.
This is really my point. I am concerned to show that Shaw was
connected with the great minds of the past who saw something
intensely meaningful in mere human existence, something important to be achieved as the result of effort, something crucial to be
exercised as the result of grace.[15]

Rather immodestly I have been speaking of Shaw as though
he did become a superman, though I mean by it only that he often
became a truly human being. Becoming human, it seems, is
nothing permanent; rather it is something accomplished only now
and then, in and out of our best moments, in keeping with a
certain rhythm. In Shaw's life, as in the lives of many people no
doubt, there is a rhythmic tensing and relaxing of the Superman
posture, corresponding to the emerging and submerging of the
vitalistic impulses of the psyche.[16] Significantly, enough of Shaw's

15. It may be helpful in understanding this chapter to have a chart of
the semantic equations it arrives at. According to their several contexts,
the following are more or less equal:

truly human＝Man＝Superman＝Super-Yahoo
merely human＝man＝Yahoo

16. In answer to the question of whether the concealed human race
will come out from under in the next thousand years, Saroyan replies:
"Well, the answer is that it is already out in myself, and we know the
slob I am, the crook, the liar, the fool, and all the other things we want
to come out from under. The habit of uselessness is strong, it persists even
after the element of the accidental in one man has enabled him or driven
him, to come out from under. And that doesn't matter. We want the
human race entire and whole. Man doesn't have to be suddenly something
different or brand-new, entirely. Just partly, just in *addition to*. And if I
have come out from under, at my best, there are surely others who have

comedy is directed against the pretensions of the Shavian Superman (Caesar's baldness) to provide a built-in safeguard against
the usurping of the personality by more extreme, Anti-Man impulses. The Anti-Man impulses are vital to the success of the
Superman efforts to become human as a kind of psychic adrenalin
to boost our merely Yahoo energies, but disaster ensues when the
Anti-Man tries to achieve otherworldly goals with only animal
strength.

As for "humanism," I have been speaking of it as though it
were all one. Far from it, there are many kinds of humanism,
which in their degree of emphasis upon the "ape" or the "angel"
in mankind may be classed as high, middle, or low. The lower
humanism insists that the ape dominates the angel in man. De-
pending upon the person, such insistence can lead to a hedonistic
indulgence of man's worst impulses (since, after all, we're "only
human"), or it can lead to a policy of rigid institutional control,
like that of the pessimistic neoclassicist. The middle humanism
aims at a more genial compromise between the ape and the angel.
Unfortunately, the theory of the harmonious man as a being in
which mind and body hold equal shares is too often sabotaged by
the practice of one or the other, ape or angel, breaking the truce
and attempting to dominate the other. The higher humanism
encourages the best in man, believing the angelic to be the true
man. The ape is not ignored, but neither is it catered to or com-
promised with. The higher humanism may seek to make the ape
work off its animal energies in behalf of angelic causes, or, more
dangerously, try to eliminate the ape altogether. In the latter case,
the higher humanism draws near to ascetic otherworldliness and
almost ceases to be humanism. A study of Bernard Shaw's novels,
I maintain, will make it clear that the humanistic tradition to
which Shaw was connected, at least early in his life, was that of
the higher humanism.

---

as well, by the thousands, most likely, although they may not be writers,
communicators, makers of influence, setters of precedents, tellers, blabber-
mouths. They may keep it to themselves, not necessarily out of selfishness
or indifference, but for want of a means by which to communicate"
(*Here Comes—There Goes—You Know Who,* p. 175).

The Emerging Superman

*The mere rawness which so soon rubs off was com-
plicated by a deeper strangeness which has made
me all my life a sojourner on this planet rather than
a native of it. Whether it be that I was born mad or
a little too sane, my kingdom was not of this world:
I was at home only in the realm of my imagination,
and at my ease only with the mighty dead. Therefore I had to become an actor, and create for myself
a fantastic personality fit and apt for dealing with
men. . . . At the time of which I am writing, however, I had not yet learnt to act, nor come to understand that my natural character was impossible on
the great stage of London.*

BERNARD SHAW
Preface to *Immaturity*

*The truth is that all men are in a false position in so-
ciety until they have realized their possibilities and
imposed them on their neighbors. They are tormented by a continual shortcoming in themselves;
yet they irritate others by a continual overween-
ing. This discord can be resolved by acknowledged
success or failure only; everyone is ill at ease until he
has found his natural place whether it be above or
below his birthplace. . . . This finding of one's place
may be made very puzzling by the fact that there is
no place in ordinary society for extraordinary individuals.*

BERNARD SHAW
Preface to *Immaturity*

Introduction

It does not take a very searching glance to see the muddle the world is in, or to see that that muddle is largely the result of the Yahoo in man. Bernard Shaw certainly was aware of the muddle at a very early age, and like anyone of sensitivity and intelligence he must have wondered how the world had gotten into it and how it was to get out. He apparently came to the usual conclusion—the conclusion that men have arrived at ever since the very first conception of deity—namely, that man as merely human cannot hope to raise himself, but must have help from some higher power. Skeptical of fatherly, omniscient deities who lived in the sky, Shaw chose to believe that the higher power man needed to raise himself resided, if anywhere, in man himself. "The kingdom of heaven is within you," he repeated. The problem was how to inspire mankind to realize the potential within itself.

I conceive of the whole of Shaw's life as a search for the god within, for the image of the divine that he as an artist could recreate in the materials of his art, to provide models of the divine image for less gifted, less imaginative people. That at least seems to be one reason why he wrote the novels in the way he did. In an 1892 review of his novels, Shaw wrote that "the business of a novelist is largely to provide models of improved types of humanity."[1] He apparently thought of the transmutation from man to Superman as an artistic process. Like an artist, the man who wishes to transmute from the Yahoo to the truly human must work from models. True enough that the Life Force itself is constantly experimenting on its own with heroic types without benefit of models, but if man is to participate in this transmutation with his contribution of intelligence and imagination, he must work from models that will exercise those faculties. Man's

1. "Mr. Bernard Shaw's Works of Fiction Reviewed by Himself," p. 238.

intelligence and imagination thus become the eyes of the Life Force, heretofore blind in its stumbling drive for godhead, and the arist is important to this drive because his faculties are specially developed.[2]

The path of Shaw's own transmutation, which presumably left behind models of improved types of humanity, I believe to be recorded in his five novels. When Shaw wrote *The Quintessence of Ibsenism* in 1891, he said that "the existence of a discoverable and perfectly definite thesis in a poet's work by no means depends on the completeness of his own intellectual consciousness of it."[3] To use one of Shaw's own favorite metaphors, what is sauce for Shaw interpreting Ibsen is sauce for the critic interpreting Shaw. Although he was a highly conscious artist, it is unlikely that Shaw was conscious of a single, unified purpose in writing his five novels; the critic who wishes to interpret them as a unified whole must take liberties with Shaw's conscious intent. In reading the novels as an autobiography of the artist's mind as it experimentally pieces together an identity, I make little attempt to determine when that mind was conscious, and when unconscious, of what it was expressing in the art of the novels.

Certainly Shaw was not aware of anything called the Superman as such (although he had read some Carlyle) until several years after the novels. Yet I believe that he was already working on the concept of the Superman in his novels, as that concept was related to his own experience. The Superman of the novels, I theorize, refers to Shaw's sense of his own uniqueness and superiority, and to his perilous attempts to be "more than man" at the risk of becoming "less than man." Those early novels' heroes

2. Jorge Luis Borges poses an interesting esthetic problem: "Can an author create characters superior to himself? I would say no and in that negation include both the intellectual and the moral. I believe that from us cannot emerge characters more lucid and more noble than our best moments. It is on this opinion that I base my conviction of Shaw's preeminence." See Borges' essay on Shaw in *Other Inquisitions, 1937–1952*, pp. 207–10.

3. Shaw, *Major Critical Essays*, p. 12.

—Robert Smith et al.—come very close to being monsters, rather than Supermen. "In trying to be more than Man, We become less," said William Blake. The novels recount Shaw's immature struggles to assert an original morality in the face of convention without losing humanity. In placing himself outside the usual definition of a human being, the moral saint invites classification with the gangster, his brother in crime. Of course the saint does not want to be criminal, nor in most cases even to be thought criminal, but the more his moral passion extrudes beyond the fixed boundaries of moral feeling called convention, the more "inhuman" he seems to others and to himself. Inhuman is a word that Shaw frequently used, ironically, to describe his superhuman heroes, indicating how sensitive he was to the accusation as well as to the danger of being inhuman.

Inhuman is the definition thrust upon the Superman from outside. The novels are worth examining, I feel, for the story of the young Shaw's attempt at self-definition. If most people are passively defined by society, Shaw at least was unwilling to accept society's definition of him as criminal. Gradually, through the novels, he interpreted his separation from society not as due to a loss of humanity but as accountable by the gift of a higher humanity, a true humanity. He was being ostracized not because he was inhuman but because he was truly human. This was a tremendous joke; but at first the Shavian hero doesn't see it. Certainly Robert Smith can see nothing funny about his predicament. By the fifth novel, however, the Shavian hero has seen the joke, accepted it, and tried to get others to see it. Shaw's strategy for getting conventional people to see the joke was to pretend to be the criminal everyone thought he was, so that the contrast between the Satanic pretension and the reality of a Christian Gentleman (i.e., a Superman) would produce a comic discrepancy.

The heroes of Shaw's novels constitute a rogues' gallery, a survey of desperate characters who terrorize respectable people with their criminal opinions. At first the hero resents his classification as criminal, then sees its comic possibilities, accepts it ironically, and develops it into a deliberate joke. This strategy is quite unlike that of the esthete who solemnly accepts his criminality as a holy trust and who ends in a tragic confrontation with the society from which he is alienated. Very much unlike "Saint Genet," "Saint Shaw" refused to remain alienated. The remark-able thing about the Shavian heroes of the novels is their deter-mined friendliness toward the society they disapprove of and which disapproves of them.

A Monster of Propriety
(Immaturity)

"I suppose you are right," said Isabella, giving him up as altogether beyond her, and raising her eyes to his with an odd mixture of ridicule and admiration. "You are such a monster of propriety *that I should be afraid to write to you even if there were none of the objections you have mentioned. Here we are at the Albert Hall. I wonder your principles did not restrain you from bringing me the longest way home."*
[emphasis added]

BERNARD SHAW
Immaturity

The delightful hero of *Immaturity*, Robert Smith, is described in terms that recall a photograph of Shaw at that age: "He was a youth of eighteen, with closely cropped pale yellow hair, small grey eyes, and a slender lathy figure. His delicately cut features and nervous manner indicated some refinement; but his shyness, though fairly well covered up, shewed that his experience of society was limited, and his disposition sensitive" (p. 4).[1] While Shaw later became a master of disguise, presenting himself as Caesar, Captain Shotover, and King Magnus, among others, in his first novel he allowed the world to get as direct a view of his essential, undisguised self as he was ever to give. There can be little doubt that Robert Smith is the proto-Shavian, the raw material out of which Shaw was later to create an astonishingly varied gallery of self-portraits.

In regard to *Immaturity*, Shaw said that "there must be a certain quality of youth in it which I could not now recapture, and which may even have charm as well as weakness and absurdity" (p. xxxix). He was right that people who did not care for his

1. Page numbers in parentheses following quotations refer to page numbers in the novel being discussed.

later work would find *Immaturity* more to their liking precisely
for those qualities of youth and charm. There is indeed a kind of
innocence in this book that is touching, and that makes the reader
feel rather friendly and protective toward the little lost dog of a
hero, Robert Smith. It is as if Smith had been dropped from the
sky, a visitor from another planet, for he is essentially parentless
and nationless. He passes for English and makes a few bitter
references to his presumably dead parents, but through most of
the novel he is without background, a homeless waif whose for-
lornness is qualified only by an obstinate spirit of independence.
We see that he is lost and that he knows that he is lost, but we are
prevented from feeling too paternal or maternal by his rather
strange way of assuming his superiority over his situation. He
does not assert his superiority, nor is he particularly aware of it;
it is just that he is quietly unexcited about *having* to assert it.
Shaw once wrote of his younger self of the Dublin days:

> I never thought of myself as destined to become what is
> called a great man: indeed I was diffident to the most dis-
> tressing degree; and I was ridiculously credulous as to the
> claims of others to superior knowledge and authority. But
> one day in the office I had a shock. One of the apprentices
> . . . remarked that every young chap thought he was going
> to be a great man. On a really modest youth this common-
> place would have had no effect. It gave me so perceptible a
> jar that I suddenly became aware that *I had never thought
> I was to be a great man simply because I had always taken
> it as a matter of course.* The incident passed without leaving
> any preoccupation with it to hamper me; and I remained as
> diffident as ever because I was still as incompetent as ever.
> But I doubt whether I ever recovered my former complete
> innocence of subconscious intention to devote myself to the
> class of work that only a few men excel in, and to accept the
> responsibilities that attach to its dignity. [p. xxxiv, italics
> added]

It is this sense of unacknowledged vocation that distinguishes
Smith from the heroes of the subsequent novels. He is much too

shy for the role of genius. "My vanity is shyness," Shaw many years later explained.[2] "Oh, if people only would be modest enough to believe in themselves," he said on another occasion.[3]

Smith's timidity, the result of an unrealized superiority, is especially apparent on social occasions. When he is invited to Hawkshaw's recital at Lady Geraldine Porter's, he greets high society "with stolidity, the effect of fright induced by his inexperience of the forms of society" (p. 299). Even after a better job has allowed him to dress in better style, Smith feels ill at ease in society and is painfully "conscious of his own deficiencies in polite intercourse" (p. 218). Smith's shyness in society can be attributed, as Shaw explained his own case, to a shortage of social drill in his youth, but the problem seems to go much deeper. When he pays an impulsive visit to Harriet at Richmond, Harriet is genuinely glad to see him. She has had opportunity to compare Smith with the grand inhabitants of Perspective, and in such a comparison Smith has gained in stature. She feels now that her former disgust with his Alhambra dancer was unfair. To make up for this injustice she greets Smith warmly and treats him to an intimate, relaxed conversation. But Smith is plagued with doubts as to his welcome. Fearing to inconvenience her, he cuts the visit short, lying to her about pressing business elsewhere. As he leaves her apartment, he berates himself for his lack of confidence: "Why should she not have been glad to see me? How stupidly I torment myself by supposing that the commonest human feelings are suspended when I am in question!" (p. 228). Shaw never really explains in this novel why Smith feels this way, and I don't think he has really adequately explained why he himself felt as Smith did. His usual explanation that his sense of inadequacy was due to mere lack of social drill, his parents never being invited out because his father was a drunkard, seems to me only a surface truth. Smith's agony after leaving Harriet's indicates something more basic. Perhaps his supposing that the commonest human feelings are suspended when he is in question

2. Allan Chaplow, ed., *Shaw the Villager and Human Being*, p. 142.
3. *Ellen Terry and Bernard Shaw: A Correspondence*, ed. Christopher St. John, p. 58.

is the result of his sense of being *uncommon*. Perhaps too that is why the boy Shaw cannot remember ever having been tendered love by his parents. How could his parents love anything so inhumanly different as Bernard Shaw? The fact about Smith, as about Shaw, that nearly overwhelms him is the fact that he is *alone*. He is alone because he is different and uncommon. The agony for Smith, as for Shaw, is that he is a very socially minded person. The importance of all this is that it provides the motive power for much of Shaw's life—the drive of the Outsider to become the Insider.

And that is why Smith is "a monster of propriety." The immature young man, unready to accept society's presumed disapproval of him, overcompensates for his sense of social inferiority by going to extremes of correctness. The point is amusingly made in several scenes with Isabella Woodward, and it is important that we notice the humor of the telling, for nothing is more characteristically Shavian than the insistence upon appreciating the humor of the situation.

In the triangular courtship among Hawkshaw, Isabella, and Smith that makes up the final book, Hawkshaw is unfavorably contrasted with Smith. Isabella, by way of Smith, had loaned Hawkshaw some jewels to pay his debts. Hawkshaw's letter of gratitude was a florid affair, "which she thought greedy in its acceptance, and fulsome in its thanks" (p. 343), betraying a weakness of character that disgusted her. Smith's letter, on the other hand, a business-like and matter-of-fact account of the rather unpleasant scene between himself and Hawkshaw, caused by Smith's insistence upon a receipt for the jewels, reveals to Isabella the unusual probity of her father's secretary, whereupon she begins "a new romance, based on respect for virtue. The figure to which she now attributed all the qualities most opposed to those of Hawkshaw was that of her father's decorous and reserved secretary. Before sunset she had imagined a phantom Smith, above all earthly passions and associations, and was abashing herself before it, and longing to lean on it for support, or by some act of self-abnegation to win its respect" (p. 343).

Isabella begins her campaign for the heart of Smith upon her return to London, and Smith, not being averse to "a snatch of innocent folly," goes along with her up to a point. But Smith's manner of conducting a flirtation is an example of exasperating rectitude. Isabella, engaged six times, has never had to work so hard for so little. One day she got him alone in a corner of a greenhouse: "She was soon alone with the secretary in a damp atmosphere of earthy fragrance, where the thermometer marked eighty degrees, and blossoms of a variety of delicate hues and fantastic shapes sprang from suspended strips of board" (p. 383). Despite Isabella's hints about Adam and Eve in Paradise, Smith imperviously discusses the ethics of the Hawkshaw affair, especially Isabella's having kept the whole thing a secret from her father. Smith had counseled telling her father, in order to get the jewels back. Isabella had never done anything so straightforward in her life, but she took Smith's advice and was rewarded by her father's reacting in the fatherly way Smith had predicted—he raged at Hawkshaw and forgave his daughter. Smith moralizes that once again virtue had vindicated its expediency. When Isabella wonderingly asks if Smith really believes that virtue is its own reward in this world, Smith cleverly replies, "If it were not . . . it would be vice" (p. 384). After an hour of such moralizing, Isabella finally leaves Smith, considering him "almost a saint because he had not behaved in the fernery as Hawkshaw would have done" (p. 387).

Smith makes a mistake, though, when Isabella persuades him to let her read his poetry, among which is the famous "To a Southern Passion Flower." Isabella naturally believes that she is the subject of that poem. The next day, so encouraged, she traps Smith in her father's drawing room. Smith uneasily comments about the "terrific weather," referring to a very heavy rain. Isabella smiles at the symbolic significance of that rain, as "she made her eyes large and lustrous" (p. 406). Suddenly feeling an urge to leave, Smith "felt the roots of his hair stir; and his knees became weak" (p. 406). When with pale face and unsteady voice he asks for her opinion of his poetry, "She was touched; for she had never seen such genuine emotion exhibited by a lover before" (p. 406). Smith is now alarmed at finding that his actions were somehow escaping his control. As Isabella pro-tests her unworthiness of the extravagant praise found in the poem, he "looked into her eyes . . . and observed, for the first time, that her eyes and hair were dark, like those of the dancer" (p. 407). She tries to egg him on by insisting that they give up this hopeless folly and become as brother and sister. When Smith eagerly agrees to that arrangement, she tries a stronger formula, calling him by his first name: " 'Well, well, be it as you will, Robert.' (Smith jumped.) 'I have no hope to give you, scarcely any heart. When next I plight my troth, it shall be as the spouse of Christ. The cloister is more peaceful; and it cannot be less happy than the world' " (p. 408). This is too much for the hu-manist Smith. He begs her not to waste her life, but she perceives that his concern is that of a humanist, not a lover. "Growing a little impatient of his scrupulously modest demeanor" (p. 409), she presses him to consider how this affair will end. Smith coun-ters by discussing his meager income, five-sevenths of which de-pends on Mr. Woodward. "It is so delightfully characteristic of you to talk about five-sevenths by way of making love," says Isabella, but "you carry conscientiousness to the most fanciful extremes" p. 409).

As the interview is about to be interrupted by another person, Smith, "hopelessly confused, could remember nothing but the gallant convention that a man who loses the chance of kissing a pretty woman is a fool" (p. 410). So he kisses her twice and flees into the night, without his overcoat and galoshes. The rain descends on him copiously. " 'Ha! ha!' he chuckled . . . 'that was not so bad for a respectable young man like Smith. He is a gayer dog than people think' " (p. 410). At home, he stands before the mirror and gazes "at the face which had won a woman's admira-tion" (p. 411). Then "Don Juan Lothario Smith" went to bed.[4]

The next morning Smith accidentally meets Isabella as she is on the way to Mass. At first he refuses to enter the "ecstasy

4. Of course when James Joyce has a man run out into the rain without his coat and galoshes, we marvel at the symbolism and the artistry. This puts us in a very embarrassing position, as everyone knows that Shaw was no artist. He was only interested in ideas.

shop," but Isabella promises the ceremony will be brief. The religious spectacle has no effect on him, except to excite his mirth and scorn of superstition. Afterwards Isabella informs him that she is obliged to travel for several months with her father and begs him to continue his suit by letter. But Smith, on his way to becoming a civil servant, expects to quit Mr. Woodward's employ and of course hopes for his recommendation. Obviously writing to her would be "impossible. I could not write to you whilst awaiting a favor from your father, knowing how he would disapprove of it. Besides, you could not write to me—at least I presume you would not care to adopt the questionable practice of writing clandestinely to a man" (p. 416). Isabella is struck dumb with amazement "at the morality of this inconceivable young man" (p. 416). When she finds her tongue, she declares him "a monster of propriety," and bids him adieu. Smith steals one last kiss and waves her goodbye. He then goes his way, "enjoying the prospect of a long respite from further lovemaking, and very far from realizing the ineptitude with which he had conducted it" (p. 417). Sometime later he receives a letter from Mr. Woodward that mentions the marriage of Isabella to another man. At this Smith gives three cheers, under his breath lest he disturb the neighbors.

And that is the substance of Smith's wonderfully humorous encounters with Belle Woodward, the point of it all being that it takes the most "immoral" of females to bring out the inconceivable morality of Robert Smith. Granted that some of Smith's morality seems put on for the sake of fending off a designing female, most of his moralizing seems quite sincere. Smith senses that Isabella, as a coquette, poses a profound threat to his propriety. In coquetry there is always the delicious sense of doing something illegal, made all the more enjoyable by the fact that coquetry is usually harmless. Smith reacts to the challenge of the coquette as would a saint—he becomes more extreme in his own rectitude. Belle Woodward's merely superficial regard for the proprieties forces Smith to defend the proprieties to the point of monstrosity, whereas with Harriet or Mrs. Froster, who insist upon the proprieties themselves, he is somewhat more relaxed in respect to these proprieties. To put it another way, Smith is more extremely moral with Isabella because in Isabella he senses a fellow "criminal," and thus is all the more eager to maintain his masquerade as a respectable person, lest he be found out by the world at large. In short, Isabella faces Smith with his greatest temptation, the temptation to drop his mask of propriety and declare himself the criminal he feels himself to be. The foolishness of Smith's monstrous masquerade is evident in view of the fact that in his sharpshooting at Isabella's Catholicism, he gives himself away anyway.

So far Smith's craving for respectability seems to be purely negative. He becomes a monster of propriety as a compensation for both his sense of inadequacy and his sense of being somehow criminal. But, as with his snobbishness,[5] his extreme drive for correctness in behavior seems to be supported by positive forces in his nature as well. Just as the snobbishness is supported by an ingrained sense of superiority, the propriety is supported by a deeply ethical nature. The trouble with Smith is that he has the natural confused with the accidental, as his author states, and thus confuses class snobbishness with individual superiority, and conventional propriety with an original morality. In this novel, unlike the novels that follow, the Shavian hero is very much concerned with meeting aristocratic standards, however republican he is philosophically, partly because these standards are institutional codifications of his own senses of superiority and propriety. He feels a natural affinity with that class which, in theory at least, shares his contempt for the base, the mean, the inartistic. He is not yet certain that this contempt is more often than not no more than a learned class prejudice, unsupported by the natural preferences of most aristocrats. The horrible Shavian truth to come is that most aristocrats, like most of the bourgeois and proletariat, are naturally common and inartistic in their preferences, and their propriety is not the result of an understanding and love of ethical principles, but only a class habit with which their real natures may violently disagree. Smith, on the

5. For examples of Smith's snobbishness, see the section "The Art of the Novels," note 43.

other hand, is all ethics. No aristocrat has ever been so scrupulous about his behavior, except in theory, and no bourgeois so
nervously insecure as to its correctness. If the monster of propriety looks like a monster from without, from within he feels
more like a timid mouse, the outward monstrosity being in direct proportion to the inward timidity.

The irony about Smith is that his extreme scrupulosity does
not win him the social acceptance he desires. To the contrary, his
extreme correctness simply makes him seem all the more unusual.
Add to this his scorn of false religion and false gentility, and
Smith finds himself very much on the outs with society. If his
"posture of opposition" makes him seem a rather stiff figure, his
extreme propriety makes him seem even stiffer. Thus, in different
ways, Smith's uncommonness forces him into the rigidity of a
mechanical monster.

Smith, however, is a very friendly monster who is puzzled by
his own monstrosity. He feels that something is wrong somewhere. From his point of view the monstrosities of the day are
to be found in Victorian social and religious practices. Yet everyone else seems to agree that the monstrosity lies in Smith. Which
is it? Smith is not at all certain, however much he likes to think
he is. If he has conviction, it is not the conviction of an Elijah or
a Jeremiah. The best he can do is argue a bit, look scornful, and
be extremely careful to avoid any improper behavior that would
support society's suspicion of his improper opinions. The discrepancy between his "criminal opinions" and his proper behavior provides a natural joke, but Smith cannot for the life of
him see it, and thus he cannot use it deliberately as the joke upon
others it really is.

Traditionally, the solution to Smith's problem has been marriage. The young man of romantic comedy who is on the outs
with society is redeemed, as society is redeemed in turn, by his
acceptance of the custom of marriage. Marriage rejoins the random individual to the social group. The random behavior of the
unmarried is replaced, theoretically, by the predictable behavior
of the married. Further, as the young man through marriage accepts the bond of common humanity, society rejoices at this new

affirmation of its collective life. The tension between the individual and the group has been replaced by harmony, and so the new
couple is sure to live happily ever after. The pattern of romantic
comedy is perfectly realized in *Immaturity* in the bourgeois marriage of Fraser Fenwick and Fanny Watkins, and imperfectly
realized in the marriage of Harriet Russell and Cyril Scott.[6]

It is well known that Bernard Shaw, always keenly aware of
the discrepancy between theory and fact, had no use for the conventional solution of romantic comedy as it pertained to himself.
He had seen too many marriages, especially that of his own
parents, belie the theory. And that is why he deliberately organized his novel in such a way as to undermine that theory. In
the marriage of Harriet and Scott, two individuals, far from
being in complete harmony with society as individuals, find
themselves more acceptable to society after their marriage than
before, in accordance with the theory of romantic comedy. But
Shaw does not ring down the curtain on this happy conclusion.
Rather he skillfully undermines the romantic comedy of the third
book by, first of all, closing it with the ghastly death of St. John
Davis, and, second, following the "courtship and marriage" of
the third book with a fourth book of inconclusive "flirtation."
The effect of the grisly conclusion to Book III and the anti-
romantic substance of Book IV is to destroy, by ironic contrast,
the sense of easy solution to Smith's problem.

6. Although the marriage of Harriet and Scott fulfills some of the
conventions of romantic comedy, it seems to reflect ironically upon others.
For one thing, in its simplicity and secularity it contrasts with the bourgeois pomp and religiosity of the Fenwick-Watkins affair. Of relevance
here is Shaw's comment in a letter to Macmillan in 1880: his design in
writing *Immaturity* was "to deal with those ordinary experiences which
are a constant irony on sentimentalism, at which the whole work is mainly
directed. The machinery employed is an arrangement of two heros and
two heroines, strongly contrasted and shuffling about, changing partners,
and playing on one another throughout. Thus, one of my alternative titles
to 'Immaturity,' was 'A Quadrille'; but I rejected it for the same reason
that led me to excise every word that betrayed the least consciousness on
my part of my own design. I also cut out pages of analysis of character,
because I think the dramatic method of *exhibiting* character the true
one . . ." (*Collected Letters 1874–1897*, p. 27).

Furthermore, the one person in the novel who in her common sense is most like Smith, and who has accepted the conventions of marriage, concludes the novel in a scene with Smith by agreeing that marriage is probably not the solution to his problem. Smith says that he "cant feel marriageable. And I doubt if I ever shall. Is marriage really a success?" Harriet replies:

"What is the use of asking that? What else is there to do if you are to have a decent home? But it is not fit for some people; and some people are not fit for it. And the right couples dont often find one another as Cyril and I did. The routine for most is, one year of trying to persuade themselves that they are happy, six months of doubt, and eighteen months of conviction that the marriage is a miserable mistake. Then they get tired of bothering themselves over it, and settle down into domestic commonplace, quite disenchanted, but not tragically unhappy. Of course, children make a great difference; but most people get tired of them, just as the children themselves do with a plaything when its novelty wears off."

"It doesnt seem to have anything to do with me," said Smith. "It may be all right; but if it did not exist I should never dream of inventing it. Goodnight." [pp. 423–24]

With marriage dismissed as a means for the Shavian monster-hero of rejoining society, and thus of achieving social identity, the hero naturally looks for other means of achieving identity. For that reason much of the novel is devoted to a discussion of vocation, as Smith struggles to achieve professional identity. Perhaps professional identity precedes social identity, since people don't know if you are acceptable to them until they know what your profession is.

One of the principal functions of Harriet in the early chapters is to draw out Smith on the topic of vocation. It seems Smith hates his job with Figgis & Weaver, "a respectable firm to whom he attributed the most sordid views of existence" (p. 11). He wonders if there is "any profession in the world so contemptible as that of a clerk" (p. 49). "He liked work; but he hated the duties of his clerkship as barren drudgery, which numbed his faculties and wasted his time" (p. 11). Furthermore, clerks being so common, the job requires a servility that challenges the cowardice of even so timid a man as Smith. It soon becomes an affair of honor to quit the job.

Smith does not quit at once, for he does not know what else he can do, and even if he knew what profession he was suited for he "couldnt afford to take it up" (p. 92). He can't go into the government because passing the civil service exam would take too much time and money. "Besides, I object on moral grounds to submit my merits to a false test. In fact, I am bound hand and foot by circumstances. I can do nothing" (pp. 92–93). This sounds very much like the early Shaw, too shy to boldly claim the role of Artist-Philosopher that is his due, evading occupation for the sake of remaining free.

In reply to Smith, Harriet engages him in dialogue on her favorite subject—succeeding in business by really trying. First she deprecates his cleverness. "You are clever enough to argue for all you do; and I fear that is all the good your cleverness will ever be to you" (p. 93). She knows from her own success "that people who set themselves out to do it can push themselves on and make their way in the world." "True," answers Smith, "but suppose it is not worth your while to set yourself out to do it. Suppose you enjoy yourself more in keeping out of the rush than scrambling in it, spending your life pushing and being pushed." "You will be left behind, and laughed at, and be sorry afterwards. Thats all," counters Harriet. Smith sees the impasse: Harriet's view of life "was a view which did not fit his temperament. Besides, the imputation of being unpractical was one which he thought he did not deserve. . . . it was elevation of taste, and not want of capacity, that had led him to contemn his daily occupation" (p. 93).

Nevertheless he admires Harriet for so resolutely becoming her own mistress and expresses his weariness of "seeing fools and irresolute creatures grovelling along in the same old track, never finding the energy to grasp their fate by the throat and lift them-

selves into a sphere of free activity" (p. 94). When Harriet
wonders why he does not apply this to himself, he assures her
that his case is quite different, although he cannot explain it. He
would quit Figgis & Weaver in a minute if he only knew what
else he was good for. This conversation reveals that Smith is very
confused by his exceptional circumstances. He is right that "his
case is quite different," but by the same token he ought to see
that he is not acting like a young man of extraordinary potential
in slavishly and timidly continuing at Figgis & Weaver. He does
not see that the new identity he wishes to carve out for himself
cannot be achieved until he breaks the mold of the clerk.

When Smith finally does nerve himself to quit Figgis &
Weaver, he discovers that there is danger in destroying an accustomed identity, for it leaves him virtually without identity
and makes him susceptible to complete annihilation of the self.
The point is made in three scenes, in Westminster Abbey, upon
a river steamboat, and in a cemetery. After storming out of the
office of Figgis & Weaver, Smith visits Westminster for the first
time in his life. No longer a common clerk, he is free to breathe
the atmosphere of greatness, and to romance about the aisles
"with the old religious sense of their peace." Avoiding the parts
of the Abbey set apart for commercial purposes, he revels in "his
seclusion from the bustle of the world." His "hushed step, impressed bearing, and reflective calm" marked him "as a confirmed
freethinker very happy." At this point the usual Shavian commonsense qualification spoils the mood with the reminder that
"As a man far removed from past ages finds romance in history
of which the persons in that history had in their time no sense,
Smith could breathe the atmosphere of the cloister with an
appreciation impossible to those whom it still overawed" (p.
166).

Then Smith boards a penny steamboat, and contemplates his
future as he flows down the river. He imagines himself in all
sorts of romantic positions—on the stage, for instance, "attired
in a fur-edged coat and hessian boots singing The Heart Bowed
Down to an enraptured audience." His common sense told him
that this was nonsense, whereupon he grew "disgusted with his

common sense, which condemned these fancies, but did not prevent their occurring to him" (p. 167).

The next day he does something even more romantic. He wan-
ders into a cemetery. His cemetery behavior is generally in the
great melancholic tradition, but graveyard irony occasionally
inspires a Shavian gaiety unbecoming to a proper melancholic.
While strolling through the multitude of tombs, he "found his
sense of the ludicrous unusually stimulated" by the comic discrepancy between the pious pretensions upon the gravestones
and the fact of death buried beneath. When he sees a woman
planting some flowers on a grave, "a perverse inclination to
laugh came upon him as he conceived the idea of the transmutation of the corpse through hideous stages of decomposition into
the very flowers she was handling with such solicitude" (p. 171).
Thus is born the Shavian habit, to some very irritating and
unfeeling, of making of death a joke.

In these three scenes Shaw is indicating, in fairly conventional
and obvious symbolism, the reaction of a sensitive young intellectual to the escape from commerce and the fact of unemployment. Smith first feels the strong pull of the cloister; then secluded
by impossibilist dreams, he floats downstream on the penny
steamer of cheap romance and finally ends in the grisly abode of
the brother of non-effort, namely death. These scenes rapidly and
effectively bring Smith to the point of return or no return. Being
Smith, he laughs at death and returns to the living with a search
for a new job.[7]

The character of Foley Woodward and Smith's becoming his
secretary are not accidental. Woodward is the personification of
Irish chaos and folly, and Robert Smith is just the man to bring

7. These three episodes reveal further that the diverse impulses of
Smith's psyche—the romantic and the commonsensical—are unresolved
except in the collision that produces his strange and rather harsh sense of
the ludicrous. This sense of the ludicrous will never entirely leave Shaw,
as it is always the source of his harsher comedy, but in later years he will
often achieve a more integrated psyche in which romance and common
sense will not constantly be at war, but rather will combine to form the
romantical common sense and commonsensical romanticism that is pecul-
iarly Shavian.

order out of that chaos and sense out of that folly. In no time at all Smith arranges Woodward's affairs so thoroughly that the work that once took all day now takes but part of the morning. So impressed is Woodward that he gives Smith increasing responsibility in handling his affairs. He allows Smith to write his one speech for that year, and finds himself consulting Smith on matters of policy. Throughout it all Smith is quietly helpful, quietly competent, a marvel of organizational genius. Though Smith continues to torment himself with the idea that he is unworthy of acceptance as a social being, he finds acceptance and identity as an efficient secretary to a Member of Parliament.

This acceptance seems to encourage Smith to pursue professional identity further, and so at the end of the novel he quits Woodward's employ for a job in the civil service. From "capitalist stooge" to private secretary for an MP to civil servant is an ominous progression, boding a Fabian future. Smith naturally gravitates toward the governmental. At the moment, however, he is curiously apolitical, the only one of Shaw's heroes that is. Part of his immaturity consists in his lack of political identity. Shaw himself did not achieve full integration of identity until his joining the Fabian society allowed him to combine his social and professional identities with his political identity. Achieving such integration is apparently what one needs to give one's being that forward thrust in a single direction which is perhaps the chief mark of a complete, mature individual. (Shaw would enjoy pointing out that this is the mark of a fanatic, as well.)

That Shaw understood this need for an integrated psyche at the time of the writing of *Immaturity* is indicated by a contrast he emphasizes between St. John Davis and Smith. Davis is euphoric in his certainty that he is one of the elect, and while Smith may classify this as arrogant humbug he is appreciative of the value of such conviction. "No doubt every man is happy who has work to do which he likes and believes in," Smith says to Davis. Davis replies that there's "plenty of the same work for every one; and youll find youll like it" (p. 22). Bernard Shaw did find that he liked it when he became the evangelist of socialism and the Life Force, but Smith is prevented by his rationalism from commitment to any creed, even the creed of Rationalism. However rationalist he may be, or thinks he is, Smith is no prophet of Rationalism.

In the preface Shaw advises us that "there will be nothing of the voice of the public speaker in [*Immaturity*]: the voice that rings through so much of my later work. Not until Immaturity was finished, late in 1879, did I for the first time rise to my feet in a little debating club called The Zetetical Society, to make, in a condition of heartbreaking nervousness, my first assault on an audience" (pp. xxxix–xl). This accounts for the curiously un-Shavian sententiousness of Smith's speech. A clue to the future, however, is to be found in Shaw's rendering of the public voice of Davis. Already he has caught the rhythms of prophetic utterance, at least in their conventional style. The eighteen-year-old Smith may feel himself incapable of such impassioned rhetoric, because it is used to convince rather than to enlighten, but the twenty-three-year-old author seems tired of his previously austere worship of Truth and yearns for the ability to sway men with the power of his eloquence. Shaw was beginning to see that it was not enough to worship Truth; he must be able to convince others that he has a vision of the Truth if he wishes to do anything effective in the world. Smith, however, is quite a way from recognizing any "call" to evangelize in behalf of a great cause. Smith is best defined, I think, by his unawareness of any special grace.

Smith is hampered in his search for identity primarily by a schism in his psyche between folly and wisdom, a schism akin to that of sense and sensibility in the debate between Harriet and Scott. Smith takes turns being wise beyond his years and foolish beneath his years. He is alternately rationalist and impulsive, commonsensical and romantic. The priggishness of his extreme rationalist posture causes him to appear somewhat foolish even in his wisdom, and he has not yet learned to be wise in his folly. Shaw will eventually come to play the role of the wise fool, as the disparate elements of his mind synthesize, but at present, rationalist that he thinks he is, Smith can see nothing wise about folly, and thus dreads making a fool of himself. "I managed by sheer perseverance to overcome my natural disinclination to make a laughingstock of myself," Shaw once remarked.[8] Significantly, Smith deprecates Foley Woodward as an "Irish jester." Smith feels nothing but shame at being the object of ridicule, even self-ridicule. His timidity and rational dignity prevent him from offering himself as a sacrifice upon the altar of laughter. Eventually Bernard Shaw learned to crucify his ego on that altar, understanding that such crucifixion was the only means of winning acceptance, but only after many embarrassing failures. Shaw found that it is easy to be foolish; it is even easy to be sententiously wise; what is difficult is to be wisely foolish.

That Smith's achievements of identity are largely negative signals the nature of his immaturity or incompleteness. Though his gravitation toward the governmental seems a positive force, actually it is more the result of a deep-seated opposition to commercial employment. Though he writes poetry, and indicates his natural affinity for the eternal society of Art by residing on Danvers Street,[9] he finds himself at odds with the conventional image of an artist as established by Perspective society. Though he considers himself a gentleman, and indeed practices propriety to the point of monstrosity, he cannot feel at home in the respectable society of Froster, Fenwick, and Watkins. Though he is a natural-born arguer for a religious cause, he can only scorn the contemporary examples of religion. Though he much enjoys the company of charming young ladies, he cannot see that the institution of marriage has anything to do with him. Though he has a lively sense of humor, the jesting of a Foley Woodward strikes him as contemptible.

Bernard Shaw did become an Irish jester, but not in the manner of Foley Woodward. Shaw did achieve gentility, but not in the manner of Fenwick and Froster. Shaw did become an artist, but not in the manner of Hawkshaw and Cyril Scott. Shaw did become an evangelist, but not in the manner of St. John Davis. Shaw did become a married man, but not in the manner of ro-

8. Winsten, *Days with Bernard Shaw,* p. 60.

9. For an explanation of the relevance of Danvers St., see the section "The Art of the Novel," note 45.

mantic comedy. Shaw, in short, managed to create a unique personality, first by distinguishing himself from those who played conventional roles, a purely negative action, and then by fashioning a positive social, professional, political, and religious identity. The basis of Smith's immaturity is that he never gets further than saying No to conventional models of artists, philosophers, evangelists, jesters, and married men. He knows who he is not, but he does not know who he is.

There is a considerable gap between Robert Smith and the heroes of Shaw's other novels. By comparison with Smith they seem extremely mature, largely because they are positive in their actions where Smith is negative. Yet Smith is by far the most real. With Smith, Shaw was looking back upon an experience of the past; with Edward Conolly and the others he was theorizing about the future. That is why if Smith is a monster he is a much less imposing fright than the others. The others are creatures of the Frankenstein brain, overstatements that have about them the queer singlemindedness of allegorical figures. While Smith's monstrosity is fully human, that of the others is rather metallic, a product of the mind's workshop. Smith is by far the most real of Shaw's heroes precisely because his author has lived him, whereas the others are would-be supermen, "models of improved types of humanity."[10] Above all else, the reader of Shaw's five novels must be aware that in passing from *Immaturity* to the other four, he is moving from experience to theory.

10. Smith's greater reality may also be accounted for by Shaw's comic treatment of him. As he wrote in the preface to *Cashel Byron's Profession,* p. vi, "The only characters which were natural in my novels were the comic characters, because the island was (and is) populated exclusively by comic characters." The heroes of his other novels are taken a great deal more seriously.

A Monster of the Mind
(The Irrational Knot)

"I envy him sometimes myself. What would you give to be never without a purpose, never with a regret, to regard life as a succession of objects each to be accomplished by so many days' work; to take your pleasure in trifling lazily with the consciousness of possessing a strong brain; to study love, family affection, and friendship as a doctor studies breathing or digestion; to look on disinterestedness as either weakness or hypocrisy, and on death as a mere transfer of your social function to some member of the next generation?"

BERNARD SHAW
The Irrational Knot

The most remarkable thing about young Bernard Shaw was his mind, and it is not surprising that he conceived of his difference from others in terms of mind. It is not surprising either that in his second novel he should focus, more specifically than in his first novel, upon the problems of possessing an unusual mind. If it was mind that made him different, then Shaw was determined to find out what that meant, for both himself and society.

Of course in all of Shaw's novels the social problem is central, for whatever the momentary preoccupation of the Shavian hero —professional, religious, political, or whatever—his constant problem is that of the unusual person's relation to his society. But in Shaw's second novel the hero is no longer puzzled or tormented by the question of his social acceptability; rather he begins to wonder if society is acceptable to him. If *Immaturity* was Shaw's *Sense and Sensibility*, then *The Irrational Knot* was his *Pride and Prejudice*. If the "pride and prejudice" of Shaw's novel is not quite true to the Jane Austen pattern, it is not merely because the object of these emotions is no more than a common

workman, but because the common workman himself feels increasingly disdainful toward the supposedly higher class into
which he foolishly marries. By the end of the novel the conventional pattern of the "pride and prejudice" sort of novel has been
completely reversed—society finds itself on the Outside looking
in enviously at the majority of one, the self-sufficient Superman. In this case the Superman is one Edward Conolly, hyper-
rationalistic inventor of the Conolly Electro-Motor.

The plot involving Conolly's encounter with high society is,
as Woodbridge says, "better ordered and more clearly focused"
than *Immaturity*'s,[1] but I doubt that this makes *The Irrational
Knot* a better novel. Since Edward Conolly is the most focused
of men, it is quite in keeping that his esthetic expression should
be continuous and single-minded. Since Conolly is the most controversial of men, it is appropriate that the concerns and conversations of the other characters should center on him. Since
Conolly is the most competent of men, it is fitting that the burden
of the novel's effective action, its forward thrust, should fall
upon him. In *Immaturity* the timid Smith was relatively easy to
overlook but in *The Irrational Knot* Conolly is impossible to
avoid—he is everywhere, making everything happen.

Once again Shaw's hero, although nominally an American, is
essentially nationless and parentless. He makes passing reference to the fact that he has "no father" (p. 59), but he never
mentions his mother. At first, while he is still impoverished and
working on his invention, he is employed in the laboratory of
Lord Jasper Carbury, an aristocrat by birth but a democrat by
temperament, who loves to tinker in his amateur way with mechanical things.[2] Lord Carbury has hired Conolly because he
respects mechanical genius, and enjoys patronizing it, in the best
sense of the word.

Conolly's first encounter with aristocracy in the novel, how-

1. Woodbridge, p. 8.
2. In revising this novel, Shaw emphasized his point about the falseness
of social stratification by changing Lord Carbury from a man more
naturally aristocratic to "a true man in a false position." See Rodenbeck,
pp. 41–42.

ever, does not take place in the laboratory. The brief opening scene shows Conolly and his sister, Susanna, at their Lambeth apartment as they are both preparing to go out for the night, Conolly to sing for a workman's benefit at Wandsworth spon, sored by Lord Carbury's wife, the Countess of Carbury, Susanna to the Bijou Theatre in Soho where she transforms into the bur, lesque queen, Lalage Virtue.

At Wandsworth Conolly proves to have musical talent supe, rior to all the performing aristocrats, for which he wins their grudging admiration. Since most of the major characters appear at this benefit, Conolly meets in quick succession the many peo, ple who will become involved in his story. He meets Marian Lind, the beauty he will eventually marry and then divorce; Nellie McQuinch, Marian's waspish friend, an extremely ad, vanced female; Marmaduke Lind, Marian's jovial, Philistine, happy-go-lucky cousin who will live illicitly with Susanna Conolly for a while; Sholto Douglas, the proud aristocrat who will first talk Marian into running away with him before aban, doning her in New York; the Reverend George Lind, Marian's dutiful and sanctimonious brother who is proud of his eloquence; and Mrs. Leith Fairfax, a busybody female novelist of decided mediocrity and irresponsible tongue.

Tired of Sholto's stiff and ceremonious courtship, Marian Lind takes a fancy to the vital Conolly and accepts his first proposal of marriage, after turning down Sholto Douglas, favored by her family.[3] Her father, Mr. Reginald Lind, nearly apoplectic at the prospect of a common workman marrying into his family, tries

3. Rodenbeck, p. 47, comments that Sholto Douglas is what much nineteenth-century fiction supposed to be a "perfect" gentleman, and thus a character of this type was often the hero. In conventional novels, the perfect gentlemen would not only succeed in his romantic endeavors, but also his opposite—the "imperfect" gentleman (Marmaduke Lind)— would come to a bad end. Shaw thus achieves irony by contrasting the frank, harmless, kind-hearted, good-natured "wickedness" of Marmaduke in his living illicitly with Susanna with the sordid, abominable, empty, minded and empty-hearted behavior of Douglas in his treatment of Marian. Marmaduke's affair, says Rodenbeck, is presented on a higher moral plane.

desperately to forestall the marriage. This incites generally amiable and dutiful Marian to walk out on her father and marry Conolly. About half of the novel is devoted to the tying of the irrational marriage knot; the other half deals with the gradual loosening and eventual untying of that knot. In *Immaturity* Shaw conceded to Victorian convention by at least marrying off the heroine, although rescuing the hero from such a fate, but *The Irrational Knot* breaks with convention entirely by making its subject a marriage in dissolution.

It seems that Conolly, a model of domestic efficiency, has left Marian "nothing to desire," whereupon she grows dissatisfied and imagines Sholto Douglas to possess all those romantic qualities she misses in Conolly. As Conolly recognizes that he has made a misalliance, he does not discourage her flirtation with Douglas. Sholto's romantical rhetoric having convinced her that the world is well lost for him, they go off on a cruise. By the time they reach New York, however, Marian has discovered that Sholto is a vacuous fraud, his aristocratic reserve having disguised a complete emptiness of mind and heart. Eventually Marian disengages herself from Sholto and prepares to abide humbly in America, in keeping with her social disgrace and what she believes to be her financial ruin.

In New York Marian conceives a "romance of penitent poverty," as one might term it, but quite unnecessarily, as Conolly has thoughtfully secured her property and money for her. Unaware that she is still a wealthy woman, Marian takes lodgings in a shabbier section of New York than her "romance of poverty" had led her to believe she would. Here she encounters Susanna Conolly, now an out-of-work performer whose alcoholism has brought her to death's door. Upon her death shortly thereafter, Conolly comes to New York to pay his last respects and to confront Marian with a decision to either return to him or not. Marian, pregnant with Sholto's child, thinks she ought not to remarry Conolly, for the sake of society. The novel ends as Conolly calmly accepts her decision and walks out.

In *The Irrational Knot*, as in all of Shaw's novels, the author was careful to arrange his characters symmetrically, as a principle of order. The rational realists are balanced off against the Philistines and idealists, and even the realists, idealists, and Philistines are arranged symmetrically within their own groups. The opening scene, for instance, is between Conolly and his sister, both rational and realistic.⁴ They balance one another in that they are at the extremes of personal control. Conolly is a monster of rational control, whereas Susanna gradually debauches herself with drink because she lacks this control. They balance too in that they present the male and female of the rational vision, just as Smith and Harriet gave common sense its male and female expressions. Since Susanna's affair is part of the subplot, and thus not often on the page, Shaw continued the balance by introducing the character of Nelly McQuinch, whose skeptic-cynic view of the world provides female balance to Conolly. Seldom does Shaw construct a scene in this novel without the presence of Nelly, Susanna, or Conolly to provide the voice of rational criticism. Even Marian in her moments of disillusionment can make sounds like a Shavian realist. (As Irvine says, "all the characters tend to become Shaws in a crisis," although the "all" makes this, like so many of Irvine's ideas, brilliantly inaccurate.⁵ In every crisis there is a very un-Shavian voice providing counterpoint.) There is balance too in the arrangement of the aristocratic idealists and Philistines opposed to Conolly. Lady Carbury and Sholto Douglas are far to the right in their regard for form, Reginald and George Lind are through their sense of accommodation to be placed somewhere near the middle, and Marmaduke and Lord Carbury through Philistine indifference and preoccupation with other practical matters are far out on the left wing.

As with Robert Smith, the character of Conolly had its inspiration in the external circumstances of Shaw's life and only gradually developed into a symbol of Shaw's inner condition as

---

4. Rodenbeck believes that Conolly's post-Ibsen "realism" was imposed upon his original "rationalism" in Shaw's later revisions. That is, the Conolly of the original version is somewhat more "rationalistic" than the Conolly of the final version, and somewhat less "realistic." See Rodenbeck, pp. 45–46.

5. Irvine, p. 27.

well. For about nine months, during the writing of the closing chapters of *Immaturity* and the opening chapters of *The Irrational Knot,* Shaw was employed by the Edison Telephone Company. Although he was the only one in the establishment who knew the theory of telephony, he was given the distasteful job of persuading people in East London to allow telephone poles on their property. When Edison merged with Bell in July of 1880, Shaw was offered a job with that firm as well, but quickly turned it down to escape the uncomfortable position of salesman. Many of the Edison Company workers were Americans, and Shaw was impressed with their practical, go-get-'em philosophy. Doubtless this experience accounted for the character and vocation of Conolly. Feeling himself unacceptable to polite society, the shabby young Shaw must have admired the contemptuous attitude of the American workers toward the useless British aristocrat. Unlike the British lower classes, the Americans showed no sense of inferiority, and indeed seemed rather to consider themselves superior to the idle aristocracy. After all, they were Workers of the World, Men of the Future, whereas the aristocrats were effete creatures, doomed to extinction. Conolly comes to see that his desire to marry a lady was sheer folly, as it causes him to marry beneath himself.[6]

Yet Shaw was always the aristocrat by virtue of his superior intellect and morality. This comes through when we discover that Conolly is not just any kind of workman; he is an inventor, and he is careful to make others see that distinction. The inventor is the aristocrat of the working classes, and his inventiveness connects him with the creativity of the artist. "I am not a scientific man: I'm an inventor" (p. 58), he says. If Conolly's being a workman is an expression of Shaw's republicanism, Conolly's being an inventor is an expression of Shaw's sense of intellectual superiority.

Furthermore, Conolly is a workman of unusual culture, due

6. In his revision for the 1905 edition, Shaw also made Conolly somewhat more consciously proletarian. As Rodenbeck says, p. 63, the 1905 version was "more clearcut in its conflicts, more powerful in its statements of contrast, and more scrupulous in its depiction of motive."

to an unusual childhood. His grandfather had been an Irish sailor with such a tremendous voice that an Italian music maestro made an opera *buffo* of him. His father was raised in Italy and became "an accompanist, then chorus master, and finally trainer for the operatic stage" (p. 16). He speculated in an American tour, married there, lost his money, then returned to England. His son, christened Edoardo Sebastiano Conolly, was left behind as an apprentice to an electrical engineer. So Conolly, like Shaw himself, was the offspring of Italian opera. This upbringing also accounts for his perfect manners; he had "learnt to dance and bow before [he] was twelve years old from the most experienced master in Europe" (p. 99). Mixing with all the counts, dukes, and queens of his father's opera company had polished his manners to perfection. And of course he could speak French and Italian fluently. Before his daughter had become infatuated with Conolly, Mr. Reginald Lind proclaimed him "Altogether a man of very superior attainments, and by no means deficient in culture" (p. 105).

It is clear that Shaw was indulging in a reaction, if not wishful thinking, in creating the character of Conolly. Conolly, the very opposite of Smith, "was about thirty, well grown, and fully developed muscularly. There was no cloud of vice or trouble upon him: he was concentrated and calm, making no tentative movements of any sort (even a white tie did not puzzle him into fumbling), but acting with a certainty of aim and consequent economy of force, dreadful to the irresolute. His face was brown but his auburn hair classed him as a fair man" (p. 3). The "modern Ben Franklin," as Conolly is called, borders on the fanatic in his pursuit of vital economy. He "never goes anywhere without an object" (p. 188) and never lets anyone waste his time. His favorite saying is one that Shaw repeated many times during his life: "There is no use in crying for spilt milk" (p. 229). There is no place for regret in a well-regulated life. When he learns that Marian has left him, he goes cheerfully to his dinner and eats a hearty meal, as becomes the inventor of that efficiency machine, the Conolly Electro-Motor, with which there is "hardly any waste" (p. 132). As Susanna says, "Ned . . . is a man in a thousand—though Lord forbid we should have many of his sort about" (p. 172). From a woman's point of view, a man who is always right is hardly bearable and something of a bore. Since he is always blameless, he has "no variety" (p. 304). Here an ominous fact needs to be noted, in explanation of the character of Conolly. It was during the winter of 1879 that Shaw met, at the Zetetical Society, that human calculating machine and future Fabian luminary, Sidney Webb. Ned Conolly is just the first of many Shaw heroes who will owe as much to Webb as to Shaw.

The authentic nineteenth-century rationalist is characterized especially by his independence of all the inefficient social ties that bind conventional people to the past—the ties of duty to church, state, or family. As Conolly says: "I am not one of those people who think it pious to consider their near relatives as if they were outside the natural course of things. I never was a good son or a good brother or a good patriot in the sense of thinking that my mother and my sister and my native country were better than other people's because I happened to belong to them" (p. 98). As for the church, in his proposal to Marian, Conolly makes it clear that he will undergo no ceremony nor allow his wife to raise his children in any one religious tradition, because he is "prejudiced against religions of all sorts." She will find him "ir-religious, but not . . . unreasonable" (p. 112). The conventions of church, state, and family are, to the rationalist, merely errors of the past made habitual. "The world would never get on if every practical man were to stand by his father's mistakes" (p. 17), Conolly informs Marian, as if to say, Progress Is Our Most Important Product.

In some respects, Conolly is an enviable man. Marian envies him and asks Douglas: "What would you give to be never with-out a purpose, never with a regret, to regard life as a succession of objects each to be accomplished by so many days' work; to take your pleasure in trifling lazily with the consciousness of possessing a strong brain; to study love, family affection, and friendship as a doctor studies breathing or digestion; to look on disinterestedness as either weakness or hypocrisy, and on death as a mere transfer of your social function to some member of the next generation?" (p. 189). The poetic Douglas replies that he could achieve all that only at the cost of his soul, a rather cheap price it turns out, as Douglas is discovered later to be completely soulless.

If Conolly is beginning to sound like Dr. Frankenstein, he has another side to him which partly redeems his scientific lack of soul. Shaw was almost incapable of creating a hero who was not in some part of him an artist. Conolly wins a grudging approval from the aristocrats by being an accomplished musician, and later he proves himself a discerning, if somewhat rationalistic, critic of painting as well. In fact, upon their marriage Marian discovers him to be a veritable monster of artistic integrity. Conolly does "not like to hear music patronized" (p. 233), and Marian gradually senses that her amateur attempts at singing and piano playing are unwelcomed by her husband. He accuses her of having "no sense at all of what was beautiful" (p. 271). Soon she stops her recitals altogether, indulging in them only when Conolly is absent.

Conolly's avocational interest in the arts causes a curious inversion in his character. Shaw was always far more of the artist than he was the man of efficiency, yet he has Conolly say, "Music is not my business: it is my amusement" (p. 15), just as, years later, Shaw would insist that his real contribution was as a Fabian, not as a playwright. But such assertions depended upon mood and audience, for he was equally adamant on other occasions that his artistic self was his greatest self. The mood of the young Shaw of twenty-four who wanted desperately to do something practical in the world was such that he created an inverted character whose practical talents are given precedence over his artistic talents, and whose rationality is given precedence over his intuitiveness.

If this inverts the real talents of Bernard Shaw, we must understand this inversion in the context of nineteenth-century estheticism and all the follies then perpetrated in the name of "Art." The fraudulent Sholto Douglas states that the true artist "instinctively hate machinery" (p. 134). In this cliché of the Art for Art's Sake school, Douglas finds consolation for his inferiority to Conolly as an artist. Like so many of his ilk, Douglas mistakes mere prettiness for art, and, unlike Robert Smith and subsequent Shavian heroes, he cannot hear the new music in the hum of electric wires or the rhythmic clicking of railroad wheels, nor can he see the new sculpture in the bassoon shape of the factory tower.[7] The Shavian artist will be a return to an older, pre-Romantic ideal, that of the stateman-poet, the man who can be both artist and practical man of affairs. Shaw refused to participate in the Romantic alienation from bourgeois society, and the lesson of his success may have encouraged the many modern artists who have found commitment to practical tasks compatible with their lives as artists. *The Irrational Knot,* however, overstates Shaw's case for the practical and the efficient.

Since with Conolly the music that is his avocation is not essential to his inventiveness, its only utility is in its therapeutic powers. Being human after all, he finds that he requires some outlet for the emotions that are otherwise so carefully controlled. The piano, organ, and voice allow him to relieve himself in politically harmless and esthetically pleasing ways. Thus Ned Conolly is an unusual rationalist, unusual in that his rationalism in no way denies the irrational. Indeed, part of his rationality consists in the sensible way in which he allows the irrational its necessary expression. When he accompanies Marian through an artistic section of the city, he jokes about taking her on his arm, a "ridiculous mode of locomotion that . . . would be inexcusable if I were a traction-engine, and you my tender." Marian sarcastically

7. In *Immaturity,* p. 120, Shaw begins a motif that will recur in his other novels. He writes that Smith, walking along the Thames, listened "to that distant rattle and shriek of trains, which had sounded to his father as the death knell of sylvan sentiment, but which was to him as characteristic of the country as the song of a blackbird. To his eye, a landscape was barren without the familiar row of white poles supporting an endless stave of music on which the insulators were the only crotchets, and which, by placing the ear against the pole, might be heard humming thunderously. Even across the Thames, and surrounded by gas works and factories decorated with tubes like colossal bassoons, they were the visible link between the maze of brick and stucco on the Middlesex side and the broad commons of Surrey and the down of the South Coast."

wants to know what people will think "if they see a great engineer violating the laws of mechanics by dragging his wife by
the arm?" Conolly replies, "I violate the laws of mechanics . . .
[because] I like to be envied when there are solid reasons for it.
It gratifies my vanity to be seen in this artistic quarter with a
pretty woman on my arm. . . . Besides, Man, who was a savage
only yesterday, has his infirmities, and finds a poetic pleasure in
the touch of the woman he loves" (p. 194). It is certainly an
unusual rationalist who can acknowledge and give sufficient play
to the savage within.

One of Conolly's, and Shaw's, favorite doctrines is that of the
holiday, a doctrine akin to that of William James'. Conolly's
favorite type of holiday is one that involves not beachball or
tennis or horse racing but flirtation. Like Robert Smith, he is
extremely susceptible to female beauty, and a pretty head can
disrupt even the most determined of his intellectual contempla-
tions. More often, however, the beauties to whom he is attracted
prove to be, like Smith's Alhambra dancer and Harriet, intellectual stimulants rather than intellectual drugs. Surprisingly,
the two women he most enjoys flirting with are Mrs. Saunders
and Mrs. Scott, the Isabella and Harriet of *Immaturity*. With
Isabella he indulges in his love of Irish jesting, with Harriet he
discusses serious matters of business, two things he never does
with Marian.

Conolly is not one to maintain the double standard, though.
He encourages Marian in her flirtations with Douglas because
"Every married woman requires a holiday from her husband
occasionally" (p. 241), and "The attentions of a husband are
stale, unsuited to holiday time" (p. 238). Marian, believing it
her conjugal duty to romance no one but her lawful husband, is
baffled by this doctrine and accuses him of not caring for her. To
her indignant question, "Do you like men to be in love with me?"
he replies, "Yes. It makes the house pleasant for them, it makes
them attentive to you, and it gives you great power for good.
When I was a romantic boy, any good woman could have made
a saint of me. Let them fall in love with you as much as they
please. Afterwards they will seek wives according to a higher

standard than if they had never known you. But do not return the compliment, or your influence will become an evil one" (p. 234). Poor Marian has been raised in the romantic tradition in which love is an all or nothing proposition, calling for complete involvement or complete indifference, and the rationalist's notion of a flirtation as a harmless play of minds is utterly beyond her.

She is further bewildered by the contradictions of Sholto Douglas. Douglas, who is convention personified in ice, hypocritically talks a different line when his own concerns are at stake. He tells Marian that conventional virtue is a hollow thing, something to be defied when it tyrannizes over the heart. "Trust your heart" (p. 258), he counsels Marian, and let us "enter on a life made holy by love" (p. 257). Uncertain of what to do, Marian discusses the problem in general terms with Conolly. Sholto has said "that to defy the world is a proof of honesty." Conolly naturally agrees. "I get on in the world by defying its old notions, and taking nobody's advice but my own. Follow Douglas's precepts by all means" (p. 260). He is practically inviting her to abscond with Douglas, for he is more concerned that she learn to be honest than with preserving a bad marriage. When, in the final scene, Marian expresses shame at having run away, Conolly rages at her for being ashamed of "the only honest thing you ever did" (p. 331).

According to Conolly, and Shaw, it is a question of education. Conventional schooling consists of teaching that the pretty theories that cover "ugly facts" are more real and more valuable than the facts.[8] Unfortunately, according to the argument devel-

8. The use of "realist," "idealist," and "Philistine" in Shaw criticism is so conventional that they probably do not require definition, but for the sake of anyone who may find it inconvenient to check *The Quintessence of Ibsenism* I include the following review. Using marriage to define his hierarchy of comic types, Shaw designated as Philistines those 700 people out of a thousand who "comfortably accept marriage as a matter of course, never dreaming of calling it an 'institution,' much less a holy and beautiful one, and being pretty plainly of the opinion that Idealism is a crack-brained fuss about nothing"; as idealists those 299 out of a thousand who devise "a fancy picture" of marriage as a "beautiful and

oped in *The Quintessence of Ibsenism,* the facts will not go away and keep tripping the idealist up. But instead of learning respect for the facts, some people, like Marian, suffer a succession of disillusionments that make no lasting impression on their deep-dyed idealism. Marian can declare on one page that love "is a myth" (p. 190), and on another page reaffirm her old idealism by stoutly maintaining that "People *do* fall in love" (p. 252). After her disillusionment with Douglas, however, she feels that the "grand passion . . . [was] a lamentable delusion" (p. 282). The novel ends in disillusionment for Marian, but as she clings to her old social idealisms in refusing to return to Conolly, the odds are good that she will restore the idealism of love before much longer. Shaw defines the idealist by his utter inability to learn from experience. It matters not how often Marian experiences the falsity of her ideals; she always returns to their defense. Conolly catalogs her crimes against the real in a lengthy, im-passioned speech that is remindful of "Don Juan in Hell":

There is no institution so villainous but she will defend it; no tyranny so oppressive but she will make a virtue of sub-mitting to it; no social cancer so venomous but she will shrink from cutting it out, and plead that it is a comfortable thing, and much better as it is. She knows that she disobeyed her father, and that he deserved to be disobeyed; yet she condemns other women who are disobedient, and stands

---

natural institution" out of fear that only by "self-denying conformity to their ideals" will corrupt human nature be held back from "ruinous excesses"; and as the realist that one person in a thousand who perceives and says that marriage "is a failure for many of us. It is insufferable that two human beings, having entered into relations which only warm affec-tion can render tolerable, should be forced to maintain them after they have ceased to exist, or in spite of the fact that they have never arisen." Further, because the idealists legislate the lives of others by insisting upon the reality of their ideals, they are inclined to either ostracize or prosecute to the death anyone who challenges their right to do so. The idealist, there-fore, although higher on the evolutionary scale than the Philistine, is the fiercest and most fanatical enemy of the realist, and will usually try to hunt him down for the noblest of reasons.

out against Nelly McQuinch in defense of the unselfishness of parental love. She knows that the increased freedom of movement allowed to her as a married woman has been healthy for her; yet she looks coldly at other young women who assert their right to freedom. [pp. 242–43]

Marian seems incapable of adjusting her conception of what marriage is supposed to be with what she has experienced it to be: "She knows that marriage is not what she expected it to be, and that it gives me many unfair advantages over her; and she knows also that ours is a happier marriage than most. Nevertheless she will encourage other girls to marry; she will maintain that the chain which galls her own wrists so often is a string of honeysuckles; and if any woman identifies herself with any public movement for the lightening of that chain, she won't allow that woman is fit to be admitted into decent society" (p. 243).

In the face of such blind loyalty to the ideal, the Shavian realist is torn between the desire to destroy the ideal and the wish to prevent anything cruel from happening to the blindfolded idealist, as one would care for a child.

There is not one of these shams to which she clings that I would not like to take by the throat and shake the life out of; and she knows it. Even in that she has not the consistency to believe me wrong, because it is undutiful and out of keeping with the honeysuckles to lack faith in her husband. In order to blind herself to her inconsistencies, she has to live in a rose-colored fog; and what with me constantly . . . blowing this fog away on one side, and the naked facts of her everyday experience as constantly letting in the daylight on the other, she must spend half the time wondering whether she is mad or sane. Between her desire to do right and her discoveries that it generally leads her to do wrong, she passes her life in a wistful melancholy which I cant dispel. I can only pity her. I suppose I could pet her; but I hate treating a woman like a child: it means giving up all hope of her becoming rational. [p. 243]

Woodbridge has suggested that the real heart of this novel is the tragedy of Marian Lind. Shaw *seems* to have agreed when he said that "The Irrational Knot may be regarded as an early attempt on the part of the Life Force to write A Doll's House in English by the instrumentality of a very immature writer" (p. xix). Considering that Shaw hadn't even heard of Ibsen at this time, the novel is remarkably similar to Ibsen's play. Conolly, despairing of Marian's ever reaching maturity, has begun to treat her more and more like a doll or a child. He never consults her on matters of serious import, not because *he* believes that women are incapable of such matters but because Marian has been trained to believe that they are, and so acts her part. But at least she is sensitive enough to know that she is being treated as a child and robust enough to resent it. She complains to Nelly that she has nothing real to do in this world: "A courtier, a lover, a man who will not let the winds of heaven visit your face too harshly, is very nice, no doubt; but he is not a husband. I want to be a wife and not a fragile ornament kept in a glass case. He would as soon think of submitting any project of his to the judg-ment of a doll as to mine. If he has to explain or discuss any serious matter of business with me, he does so apologetically, as if he were treating me roughly" (p. 202).

Nelly points out that she didn't like the other approach either. When Conolly tried to treat her as a rational adult, she imme-diately took refuge in childish idealisms. This novel may be Shaw's A Doll's House, but Conolly has nothing in common with the husband of Ibsen's Nora. In a way, Shaw's version is a reply to Ibsen in that he shows what happens to Nora after she slams the door. Marian, like Nora, has been trained to behave like a doll, and though she is intelligent and robust enough to rebel against this, the training is deeply ingrained. Her tragedy is summed up in the old formula of realism's favorite melodrama— the heroine caught between two worlds despises the one that she is born to, yet the one she longs for she has not really been prepared for and is quite powerless to bring into being.

Shaw effectively symbolizes Marian's fate through the de-vice of a dream. The dream occurs after Marian has just encountered the drunken Susanna in the shabby New York lodging house, and has been forced to make the galling and humiliating confession that she was an unfaithful wife to Susanna's brother. That night Marian dreams "that she was unmarried and at home with her father, and that the household was troubled by Susanna, who lodged in a room upstairs" (p. 305). Marian and Susanna end up in the same lodging house because they are really "sisters" underneath it all and belong in the same house of disrepute. Even in her dream house, Marian cannot restore the ideal without a sense of the troubling presence of Susanna's reality, just as respectability depends upon the troubling presence of the disreputable for its *raison d'être*. You can't have repute without disrepute. The dream signifies that the "good" Marian senses, at least unconsciously, her complicity in the fate of her "evil sister." There is irony, further, in that Susanna, a faithful if illegal wife, destroys nothing but herself; whereas Marian in her idealism manages to mar the lives of half a dozen others including Susanna. It is no wonder that in the escapist world of the dream, Susanna has become a difficult boarder in the house of the ideal.

Nelly McQuinch is perhaps better prepared for the brave new world of women's emancipation, but in the present world of assumed female inferiority she is quite a misfit. She is tolerated by Mr. Lind only because her cynicism serves as a correction to Marian's extravagance. Nelly asks, "What is the use of straining after an amiable view of things, Marian, when a cynical view is most likely to be the true one." "There is no harm in giving people credit for being good," replies Marian, whose eyes always plead for peace like a good angel. Nelly disagrees: "Yes, there is, when people are not good, which is most often the case. It sets us wrong practically, and holds virtue cheap" (p. 62). This is the general pattern of the many particular conversations between the two girls. Nelly has a sharp eye for the flaws in reality, and, as she says, "my disposition is such that when I see that a jug is cracked, I feel more inclined to smash and have done with it than to mend it and handle it tenderly ever after" (p. 205). Marian of course would normally try to mend it, or pretend the crack wasn't there, but she is married to a husband who has the same intolerance of cracked jugs. Conolly forces her to break the cracked jug of their marriage and start over.

It is Nelly who forces Marian to break the cracked jug of the parental relationship. When Mr. Lind fails to back Marian in her choice of Conolly, Nelly advises her that she is fighting "the most unreasonable of adversaries, a parent asserting his proprietary rights in his child" (p. 151). Nelly has good reason to know about such adversaries, as much of her childhood was spent combatting the wrong-headed tyranny of Mr. and Mrs. McQuinch. The McQuinches believed that "when God sent children he made their parents fit to rule them." Unfortunately the McQuinches were no more fit to have charge of Nelly "than a turtle is to rear a young eagle" (p. 32). In this novel, says William Irvine, "the respectable mantle of John Stuart Mill is lifted and the cloven hoof of Samuel Butler becomes visible."[9] Shaw had not heard of Butler at this time, but the McQuinches do indeed seem to be close neighbors of Butler's Pontifex family.

And it is Nelly who envies the independence of Susanna Conolly. Nelly has come to see that marriage is just the polite word for legalized prostitution, and she admires a woman like Susanna who has the spunk to live outside that institution. When Susanna shocks Marmaduke by rejecting his offer of a clandestine marriage and insists upon remaining independent by paying her own way, Marian is scandalized. But Conolly wants to know: "What has Susanna to lose by disregarding your rules of behavior? . . . She would not really conciliate you by marrying, for you wouldnt associate with her a bit the more because of her marriage certificate. . . . Believe me, neither actresses nor any other class will trouble themselves about the opinion of a society in which they are allowed to have neither part nor lot" (pp. 98–99).

However much Conolly defends Susanna's right to live her private life as she chooses, he is contemptuous of her choice of public life, of the way she has prostituted her talents on the burlesque stage as Lalage Virtue. When she is dying the slow death of the alcoholic, her performance deteriorating proportionately, Conolly advises her to hurry up and die if she is bent on killing

9. Irvine, p. 26.

herself. The shocking part was not that he gave that advice but that it was "the very best advice he could have given" (p. 231). Susanna believes that she didn't make herself nor her circumstances and, when Ned visits her death bed in New York, he seems to at least partly agree. To Marian he explains her motive for drunkenness:

> Society, by the power of the purse, set her to nautch-girl's work, and forbade her the higher work that was equally within her power. Being enslaved and debauched in this fashion, how could she be happy except when she was not sober? It was her own immediate interest to drink; it was her tradesman's interest that she should drink. . . . She was clever, good-natured, more constant to her home and her man than you, a living fountain of innocent pleasure as a dancer, singer, and actress; and here she lies, after mischievously spending her talent in a series of entertainments too dull for hell and too debased for any better place, dead of a preventable disease, chiefly because most of the people she came in contact with had a direct pecuniary interest in depraving and poisoning her. [pp. 332-33)]

The shock of seeing his sister's dead body forces Conolly to abandon his kid-glove treatment of Marian. He calls for "an end of hypocrisy! No unrealities now: I cannot bear them. Let us have no trash of magnanimous injured husband, erring but repentant wife. . . . Now I refuse all conventions" (p. 331). He speaks harshly to her about her self-deception, and she is surprised by this rough treatment from one who has always treated her as a doll before. She accuses him of not being himself, and he replies, "On the contrary, I am like myself—I actually am myself tonight. . . . Is it utterly impossible for you to say something real to me?" (p. 332). When Conolly offers to take her back and be a father to Sholto's child if only she will snap her fingers at the social disgrace that is sure to meet her in London, Marian is still bound fast by her well-trained sense of duty. She thinks that she had better remain "free" and "independent," and she is baffled by Conolly's willingness to give up his freedom to take on a family again.[10] At this Conolly makes a very Shavian speech:

> Freedom is a fool's dream. I am free. . . . I once thought, like you, that freedom was the one condition to be gained at all cost and hazard. My favorite psalm was that nonsense of John Hay's:
>
> > For always in thine eyes, O Liberty,
> > Shines that high light whereby the world is saved;
> > And though thou slay us, we will trust in thee.
>
> And she does slay us. Now I am for the fullest attainable life. That involves the least endurable liberty. You dont see that yet.[11]

This is a curious definition of liberty, a definition that leads straight to Karl Marx (or to Roman Catholicism in other cases). It was Shaw who insisted on the paradox that socialism was resisted because it offered people too much freedom. People supposedly found it much easier to be wage-slaves than to run their own society.

That people love to call their slavery "freedom" is illustrated by the way Marian is bound by social duty to remain free of Conolly. Furthermore, she does not even have the usual consolation of disappointing Conolly by refusing him and nobly remaining true to her duty, for Conolly has foreseen how he would adapt himself to that circumstance. He always faces facts. " 'You are too wise, Ned,' she said. . . . 'It is impossible to be too wise, dearest,' he said, and unhesitatingly turned and left her" (p. 336). More explicitly than the negative shake of the head that ends *Immaturity*, this exchange between Conolly and Marian that concludes *The Irrational Knot* dismisses the conventions of

10. Rodenbeck, p. 49, writes that Marian's "refusal to go back to him is . . . less an acceptance of the challenge of ultimate freedom than a submission to the rule of society; she has already . . . been declassed by her adultery."

11. *The Irrational Knot*, pp. 334–35. The earlier *Our Corner* version reads: "Now I aim at the greatest attainable justice, which involves the least endurable liberty."

society as delusions not to be countenanced by the rational mind.

Critics have been hard put to know what to make of Edoardo Sebastiano Conolly. Woodbridge believes that the lesson of the novel "is that a man who tries to become a purely rational think-ing and acting machine will wreck his own life and other peo-ples'."[12] While Shaw may have intended a "tragic" conclusion, he surely would not have agreed with the implication that Conolly could and should have averted this ending by being more "human." If the conclusion really is tragic, then that means it could not have been averted. The collision between the irra-tional world and the rational man must end in catastrophe, as the rational man must be what he is and the irrational world must remain what it always has been. But I have an eerie feeling that Shaw does not mean for us to judge Conolly's life as wrecked. Quite the contrary, this experience with the untying of the irra-tional knot has left him stronger and more vitally aware than ever before. The conclusion leaves us with the sense that Conolly will go on to great things because the encounter with Marian, as a test of himself, has merely served to reveal himself to him-self, making him all the more confident of his own strength and quality of mind. Conolly is far from being a tragic figure.

In fact, tragedy is extremely rare in Shaw's world. Just as it has been argued that there is no such thing as Christian tragedy because the saint ultimately triumphs over his martyrdom, so too "Shavian tragedy" seems to be a contradiction in terms, for in the little catastrophes that fall upon the Shavian hero there is usu-ally the sense of ultimate triumph. The difference is that with the Shavian hero the triumph of the indomitable spirit is expected to occur in this world. Apparently Shaw was constitutionally in-disposed to see himself as a tragic figure. Only in *Saint Joan* and perhaps in *Heartbreak House* did he allow a moment of tragic mood. He avoided Socrates and Jesus and wrote instead about the superman conquests of Napoleon and Caesar, Caesar's play ending before the return to Rome and the assassination. He wrote a playlet dealing with the trial of Jesus, but cut it off before the crucifixion.

12. Woodbridge, pp. 8–9.

Saint Joan proves that Shaw did not lack tragic insight; and that he consciously strove to avoid martyrdom by creating the character of the Shavian fool proves that he was fully aware of the tragic potential inherent in the career of the Socratic gadfly. But if Edward Conolly is not a tragic figure, neither is he a comic figure, a "wise fool," for he dislikes being the butt of the joke as much as did Robert Smith. In Conolly's opinion, says Marian, "the greatest misfortune that can happen to any one is to make a fool of oneself" (p. 199). Making a fool of oneself is the mark of idealism and ignorance, the twin sources of the irrational in human affairs, and naturally no self-respecting rationalist would allow himself such foolish postures. For Conolly folly is something that is indulged in out of weakness, not a strategy for wisdom. In these early novels, the part of the fool is always given to a minor character. In this case, Marmaduke lightens the tone of the book with his "gift of drollery."

Conolly is still a monster of propriety, in his own way even more so than Robert Smith. But now the propriety is not confused with an external social system, rather it develops more intensely into a private, internal sense of the correctness of certain human conduct. Shaw, as much as Hemingway, possessed a private code of conduct which he expressed literarily in the conflict between the Shavian hero and the people who follow an external code. The Shavian hero, like the Hemingway hero, carries the code around inside him, and of course others constantly violate it because they don't know it's there. The others see only what appears to be a lawless man, who gets extremely irritated whenever they cross him by following their conventions. "They get on with the queerest makeshifts for self-respect," says Conolly, "old Mr. Lind with family pride, Douglas with personal vanity, and Marmaduke with a sort of interest in his own appetites and his own jollity. Everything is a sham with them: they have drill and etiquette instead of manners, fashions instead of tastes, small talk instead of intercourse" (p. 270). In fact, the more mannerly the Shavian hero is, the more unmannerly he seems to those who consider personal manners to be synonymous with an impersonal system of etiquette.

This confusion between the real and the ideal is most humor-
ously illustrated by the results of the Reverend George Lind's
visit to Conolly's sister. When Reverend Lind, feeling "like St.
Anthony struggling with the fascination of a disguised devil"
(p. 169), pays a visit to the voluptuous Lalage Virtue, who
meets him dressed in a harem costume, he informs her that if
Conolly marries Marian she must give up her illicit relationship
with Marmaduke, as the scandal of it would then reflect on
Marian. After a dazzling display of intellect in which Susanna
inverts all his values, somehow managing to put him in the
wrong, she seductively contrives to fall into his arms. At this the
much distraught Reverend hastens home and composes a sermon,
the general theme of which is "How can Satan cast out Satan?"
Reverend Lind is referring specifically to the way people visit
the Baal-altars of local theaters hoping to cast out their devils
through the pursuit of pleasure, which of course is Satanic; but,
more generally, he refers to the fact that "there is not left in
these latter days a sin that does not pretend to work the world's
salvation, nor a man who flatters not himself that the sin of one
may be the purging of many" (p. 184). If you are a devil, yet
claiming to have cast out many devils, the Lord scoffing shall say,
"How can Satan cast out Satan?" It is an interesting question,
made even more interesting by Shaw's asking it at the beginning
of his Satanic career.

Shaw does not answer it directly in this novel, but it is im-
plicit in everything he wrote. The answer is that the conventional mind, like that of Reverend Lind, has allowed appearance
primacy over reality. It has failed to see through the Satanic
disguise, preferring formal piety to real piety, just as it prefers
formal etiquette to real manners. This preference for illusion is
best exemplified in the primacy of word over thing. "The Atheist," complains Reverend Lind, "no longer an execration, an
astonishment, a curse, and a reproach, poses now as the friend of
man and the champion of right" (p. 184). It matters not that an
Atheist might be the most godly man living, the important thing
to Reverend Lind is the *word* Atheist, which he superstitiously
capitalizes. That word qualifies the man as Satanic and thus dis-

qualifies him from casting out Satan. To bring attention to this confusion, Shaw spent a lifetime masquerading as Satan while behaving, in his own fashion, like Christ, just as Christ himself in scourging the Pharisees must have looked to the Pharisees more like Satan. To make his point obvious, Shaw played Satan as a joke, and it is amazing the number of people who never "got it."

Shaw explains in his preface (p. vi) that while writing *The Irrational Knot* he used Bizet's *Carmen* "as a safety-valve for my romantic impulses. When I was tired of the sordid realism of Edward Conolly . . . I threw down my pen and went to the piano to forget him in the glamorous society of Carmen and her crimson toreador and yellow dragoon. . . . The Carmen music was . . . exquisite of its kind, and could enchant a young man romantic enough to have come to the end of romance before I began to create in art for myself. I still could enjoy other people's romances."[13] Although the later Shaw did not find Conolly's realism quite so sordid, nor Bizet's *Carmen* quite so attractive, this confession shows us how far the young Shaw was from accepting rationalism as his ideal. Indeed there seems to be implied criticism in the fact that Conolly's two-year marriage was childless, whereas Marian's short episode with Douglas was quite fertile. This can be construed as a comment on "barren rationalism," if you like. On the other hand, Shaw may have been saying something more complex. Conolly is creative enough in the world of ideas, and thus his fertility is to be measured not in children produced but in inventions completed. That Marian cannot conceive by him may be no more than a comment upon the incompatibility of realist and idealist.[14] Furthermore, there

13. Incidentally, in "Mr. Bernard Shaw's Works of Fiction Reviewed by Himself," Shaw writes that "long before I got to the writing of the last chapter I could hardly stand [Conolly] myself" (p. 239).

14. In "Mr. Bernard Shaw's Works of Fiction Reviewed by Himself," p. 239, Shaw writes of his principal characters: "My model man, named Conolly, was a skilled workman who became rich and famous by inventing an electro-motor. He married a woman whom I took no end of trouble to make as 'nice' as the very nicest woman can be according to conven-

is poetic justice in Marian's romantic "conceptions" turning out
to be fraudulent and bastardly, as symbolized by the impregnation of her by Sholto Douglas. As Douglas absconds, and romance disappears, Marian is left with the reality of a child.
Romance is undoubtedly more fertile, but in the end the children
it produces are very real, and bastards at that. Note that it is
Conolly the realist who is willing to raise the bastard as his son.

And it is Conolly's realism that often rescues him from his
own mere rationalism. As I have said, Conolly, unlike the rationalist of convention, is unusually aware and indulgent of the irrational. He would agree more than anyone with Marian's idea
that we should not let "our little wisdoms stifle all our big instincts" (p. 253). He congratulates her for having done the
honest thing in running off with Douglas. This burst of honesty
encourages him in turn to allow freer play to certain of his own
impulses. At the beginning Conolly is much like Smith in following a surface propriety in his treatment of Marian. He practices
a kind of deception, the kind that adults use on children to pro-
tect them from what the adults conceive to be "harsh realities."
But in the final scene he breaks loose from this habit of treating
idealists like children and begins the tactic of expressing honestly
his sense of the real. Idealists are no longer to be pampered or
catered to; their only chance of growing up is to be told the truth.
In keeping with his need to follow his own "big instincts," the
Shavian hero now enters on a period of rudeness and social impropriety, as we shall see in the next novel.

---

tional ideas. The point of the story was that though Conolly was a model
of sound sense, intelligence, reasonableness, good temper, and everything
that a thoroughly nice woman could desire and deserve, the most hopeless
incompatibility developed itself between them. . . ."

A Monster of the Body
(Love Among the Artists)

*I exhausted rationalism when I got to the end of my
second novel at the age of twenty-four, and should
have come to a dead stop if I had not proceeded to
purely mystical assumptions. I thus perhaps destroyed my brain, but inspiration filled up the void,
and I got on better than ever.*

BERNARD SHAW
Letter to
the Abbess of Stanbrook

Looking back from the present, it is easy to see what Shaw was
driving at in *The Irrational Knot,* but for the author himself at
the time of writing things must have seemed less clear. The young
Shaw thoroughly understood that the negativism of Robert
Smith led nowhere, that the "posture of opposition" had to be
replaced by a "posture of proposition"; but what the posture of
proposition should be was not at all clear. In his deep need for
positive action, a need quite as fundamental as his need to oppose, Shaw attempted in *The Irrational Knot* to convert conventional rationalism from a nay-saying agnosticism to a yea-saying
religion of rational realism.[1] He managed well enough to give
Conolly the appearance of a religiously motivated man, but he
did not succeed in converting Conolly's rationalism into a religion. Instead he ended up with a puzzling discrepancy between
the religious force of some of Conolly's actions and the total
absence of a religious motivation, a religious theory that would
explain those actions. That is, Conolly at times *acts* like a man
with a holy cause, but nowhere in the novel is that holy cause

1. In interpreting Shaw's use of the word "realism," one must keep in
mind that in *The Quintessence of Ibsenism* his primary examples of realists were Shelley and Plato. The reality that Shaw had in mind was not
that of the cynic but that of the poet.

stated. Certainly the cause is not rationalism, for that part of Conolly is the anti-religious part, the purely destructive part, the part that insists upon breaking cracked jugs.[2] If, therefore, readers of *The Irrational Knot* wondered what the deuce made Conolly so confident of himself, it is not surprising, for there is no adequate reason given.

Shaw later came to a much different understanding of his mind, an understanding that provided a built-in religious motivation. He came to see that it was not his extreme rationality that made him different from others, but rather the passion of his moral genius and the inspiration of his artistic genius, both gifts and instruments of the Life Force.[3] The mind of the Shavian hero continues to be rational, because, as Shaw says in *The Quintessence of Ibsenism*, "ability to reason accurately is as desirable as ever; for by accurate reasoning only can we calculate our actions so as to do what we intend to do: that is, to fulfil our will; but faith in reason as a prime motor is no longer the criterion of the sound mind, any more than faith in the Bible is the criterion of righteous intention."[4]

Critics whose minds run along the grooves of cliché have tended to label Shaw and Shaw's heroes as "coldly rationalistic," because reasoning is supposed to be mechanical and machines are supposed to be inhumanly cold. But all of Shaw's heroes, even the ones who think they are cold-hearted rationalists, possess minds chiefly characterized by the intense heat of their visions of the real, visions which consist of a sort of rapid reasoning about events and issues. Of Saint Joan, for instance, Shaw wrote that "everything she did was thoroughly calculated . . . though the process was so rapid that she was hardly conscious of it, and

2. Henderson, p. 43, quotes Shaw to the effect that "religion is that which binds men to one another, and irreligion that which sunders. . . ."

3. Shaw's remark about the "moral passion" that occurred to him in his mid-teens is well known, but perhaps less famous is his assertion that his second novel was "one of those fictions in which the morality is original and not ready-made. Now this quality is the true diagnostic of the first order in literature, and indeed in all the arts, including the art of life" (*The Irrational Knot*, p. xvii).

4. *Major Critical Essays*, p. 22.

ascribed it all to her voices. . . ."⁵ This rapid reasoning amounts to the sort of instantaneous perception of reality that is conventionally called vision. The point to be made is that there is nothing cold or mechanical about this rapid reasoning. With its source in the irrational unconscious, which presumably contains the entire past of the Life Force as well as its present impulses and the potential of its future, this superrational vision is more like a hot, flashing light that, passing through the mind, illuminates some of the dark places. In no joking mood, Shaw once compared this action of the mind to sexual orgasm, to the detriment of the latter. He had come to understand that blood is the very life of the brain and that the mind is therefore an organ of passion as surely as any other organ of our bodies.⁶

Conventionally, however, passion has been considered a function purely of the body (or the "heart," as certain female novelists of Shaw's day would have insisted), just as reason has been considered a function purely of the mind. In his art, therefore, Shaw used the mind and the body as conventional symbols of the rational and the irrational, though he also used them unconventionally to make the point that the usual dichotomy was not accurate. Of course he did not deny that the body was partly the source of the irrational, but he did insist that the mind contained a greater part of the irrational, a vastly more important part, and perhaps a part that determined the irrationality of the body. At any rate, the only way he could see to make this point in literature was by first accepting the conventions, i.e., by using the body to symbolize the irrational, and then by using the body to symbolize the irrationality of the *mind*.

In Shaw's third novel, *Love Among the Artists,* the hero as a monster of the body symbolizes Shaw's extreme turn to the irrational, after becoming fed up with Conolly's equally extreme rationalism. The hero is one Owen Jack, a composer modeled on Beethoven, as far as looks, manner, and temperament are con-

5. Bernard Shaw, *Saint Joan* (New York: Dodd, Mead, & Co., 1963), II, 283.

6. For a further development of this idea, see my article "Shaw and the Passionate Mind," *The Shaw Review* (May, 1961), pp. 2–11.

cerned.[7] In his compositions, however, Jack is post-Wagner, thus the scorn and obloquy heaped upon him by the academies who will allow nothing past Beethoven to be called music. A major theme is the obvious one of genius neglected and genius ultimately vindicated. The point is made repeatedly by contrasting the authentic genius of Owen Jack with the uninspired craftsmanship of Adrian Herbert, a contrast echoed on the female side by the difference between Madame Szczympliça, a Polish pianist of international renown, and Mary Sutherland, a mere dabbler in art.

The title of the novel is supposed to be a humorous reminder of the old popular song, "Love Among the Roses," but it is misleading if it suggests Bohemian love affairs. Rather than being centered on love, the novel is concerned with art first, and whether artists should let love divert their energies second.

The plot of the novel is more complicated than that of *The Irrational Knot,* but its structure is fairly simple.[8] The novel has two books—the first very long, the second very short—which, although without titles, might be called "Before Marriage" and "After Marriage." In the opening scene we find Owen Jack sitting on a park bench in Kensington Gardens, to which Mary Sutherland, her father, and Adrian Herbert have come to view

7. As Pearson puts it, p. 57, Jack "was the first of a line of historical characters whose imputed share in Shaw's powers of entertainment makes them a good deal more pleasant than the originals could have been."

8. Henderson, p. 98, enjoys saying that the novel is "as innocent of plot as a Sunday school tract," but, as is so often the case in Shaw criticism, the enjoyment comes at the expense of understanding. Henderson seems to have been unable to reconcile himself to any plot that was not mechanical and contrived. Shaw perfectly describes the sort of plot Henderson had in mind in his ironic disavowal of plot: "I can guarantee you against any plot. You will be candidly dealt with. None of the characters will turn out to be somebody else in the last chapter: no violent accidents or strokes of pure luck will divert events from their normal course: forger, long lost heir, detective, nor any commonplace of the police court or of the realm of romance shall insult your understanding, or tempt you to read on when you might better be in bed or attending to your business" (Woodbridge, p. 11).

the Albert Memorial. Fatigued, they share the bench with Jack, a stranger to them, and in the conversation discuss the trouble they've had getting a tutor for Charlie, Mary's younger brother. Jack, impoverished as usual, astounds them by butting in to offer his services as tutor. Herbert and the Sutherlands are taken aback by the impropriety of this, but promise to check his references. Jack is eventually hired for the post, and gets along famously with Charlie. Unfortunately, Jack's rough manner and brutal attacks upon the pianoforte in his labors of composition constantly offend the delicate sensibilities of his employers, causing his dismissal.

On the train back to London, Jack encounters Mr. Brailsford and his daughter, Madge, acquaintances of the Sutherlands. Brailsford is a haughty, intolerant old man who tryannizes over his daughter, a spirited girl who wants to go on the stage. Brailsford has a secret love for the stage himself, but since acting is not a respectable profession for a lady he cannot allow it. Jack and Brailsford pass the time exchanging insults and anathemas, until upon reaching London Jack aids Madge in escaping from her father. Later, à la Professor Higgins, Jack instructs Madge in elocution, the first step in her slow progress in becoming a queen of the theatre.[9] Mr. Brailsford eventually becomes reconciled to his daughter's choice of profession, but only after a bitter interval of disowning her. Finally, after Madge establishes herself as a first-rate actress, she attempts a liaison with her Pygmalion, but Jack rebuffs her.

The rest of the novel is largely concerned with Jack's rise to fame, his conflict with the academicians, and especially with the contrast between the two geniuses, Jack and Madame Szczympliça, and the two would-be artists, Mary Sutherland and Adrian Herbert. The contrast is made by a familiar Shavian device, that of misalliance. The characters engage in a sort of dance in which

9. According to R. F. Rattray, Shaw met an old Alsatian opera singer named Deck in 1880 who gave him much the same elocution lessons that Jack gives to Madge. Deck also encouraged Shaw to bank up his hair for Satanic effect (*Bernard Shaw: A Chronicle*, p. 39).

various partners are tried, found incompatible, and exchanged for other partners.

Mary Sutherland begins the series of exchanges when she discovers after a long engagement to Adrian Herbert that despite their kindred interests in art she does not really wish to marry Adrian. Adrian, having become infatuated with Madame Szczymplica, feels much the same way. The engagement is broken off, Adrian marries Madame Szczymplica, and Mary ultimately marries a Mr. Hoskyn, a promoter for the Conolly Electro-Motor. Before Mary settles for Hoskyn, however, she is proposed to by Owen Jack, who in a moment of weakness had tried to mix marriage with art. He is rescued by her refusal and dedicates himself thereafter to a life of art. Aurélie Szczymplica had not been so lucky. Aurélie finds her marriage to Herbert a great inconvenience to the pursuit of her art, the problem being solved only by leaving Herbert behind when she goes on tour. Herbert meanwhile has become such a slave to his love that he grows negligent in his painting. In all this the only really successful and healthy marriage is that of Mary and the Philistine mechanic, Hoskyn, who succeed largely because they never interfere in one another's business. That genius should not marry is obviously the moral. Genius should especially not marry mere Talent. Talent would be much better off allying itself with Business Interest and Practical Efficiency.

In *Love Among the Artists,* says Pearson, Shaw abandoned rationalism and "took for his theme the degrees and contrasts of that entirely mystical (or superrational) thing called genius."[10] Shaw believed that his reaction against Conolly was total: "Jack is just the opposite of Conolly: the man of genius as opposed to the rational man. The novel makes a *volte face* on my part. I had before kept within intellectual bounds: here I let myself go and guessed my way by instinct."[11] But Shaw is here confusing fact with theory, for the reaction against Conolly was not so absolute as he would have us believe.

I have already shown that while Shaw may have intended

10. Pearson, p. 58.
11. Rattray, p. 39.

Conolly to be the complete rationalist, he rather failed by making the man something of an artist and something of a genius as well. The factual character does not fit the theoretical character. The same is true of Owen Jack. However hard Shaw tried to present the character of willful, abandoned genius, he succeeded only in creating another Shavian hero who partakes of his creator's unusual combination of sense and sensibility. The difference between Jack and Conolly is one of degree, not the one of kind that Shaw would have us believe.

Jack tries very hard to be the opposite of Conolly—"I hate business and know nothing about it" (p. 16)—but he drives a good bargain with the Sutherlands for his tutorship, and calculates to the penny the money he impetuously gave Madge at the train when she was escaping from her father. When Madge comes to repay it, Jack does not refuse it, he simply refuses to touch it and has her hand it to his landlady, Mrs. Simpson. Jack's impulses are all magnanimous. He gives Madge elocution lessons for free, but poverty makes him conscious of the need for some efficiency in money matters. The impecunious young Shaw must have decided that poverty is the natural condition of genius. That accounts for the name of his hero. Owen Jack is always owing "jack." It's "a fit name," says Mrs. Simpson, although she concedes that he is "honorable when he has the means" (pp. 66–67). It must have been aggravating for the efficient young Shaw not to have any money to be efficient with. Of course if you don't have any money to be efficient with, the next best thing is to show your contempt for it, and this Shaw did, without much conviction, by drawing the character of Jack.

Jack is like Conolly in other ways. Jack is no mechanic, but he shares with Conolly and every other Shaw hero the appreciation of the machine. On the train ride to London, Jack is exhilarated at the rhythmic clattering of the wheels and composes in accordance with their inspiration. At the first playing of Jack's *magnum opus*, "Prometheus Unbound," Adrian Herbert is disgusted by the total lack of melody, whereas the American mechanic, Mr. Hoskyn, thinks it a wonderful piece of music because it "reminds [him] of the Pacific railroad" (p. 245). Later, at Lady Geraldine's, Conolly the mechanic plays some of Jack's music "much more calmly and accurately than Jack himself played it" (p. 230). Noting the use of the comparative, it is, as I said, a matter of degree.

Jack is perhaps most unlike Conolly in his social manner. To Mr. Brailsford Jack says, "I am as well versed in the usages of the world as you; and I have sworn not to comply with them when they demand a tacit tolerance of oppression. The laws of society, sir, are designed to make the world easy for cowards and liars. And lest by the infirmity of my nature I should become either the one or the other, or perhaps both, I never permit myself to witness tyranny without rebuking it, or to hear falsehood without exposing it" (p. 46). Conolly would agree with this diagnosis of the laws of society, but he's far too civilized, except in the final scene with Marian, to conduct a deliberate campaign of insulting people. He is normally urbane and tactful in his truth-telling. Not so Owen Jack, who is variously described as "a bear," "a bull," "a buffalo." When conducting the orchestra of the Antient Orpheus Society, he castigates them for being "over civilized . . . afraid of showing their individuality. . . . It was written to be played by a savage—like me" (p. 138).

Long before Eliot's Prufrock and Joyce's James Duffy, Shaw understood that an effective personality must descend into the brute irrational for the source of its energy. Furthermore, he came to believe that a truly whole personality was an evangelistic personality, devoted to attack and conversion. Truth was the result of conflict, a strife of wills, and it took something of the animal to engage the enemy, however intellectual the combat. That is why the hyper-civilized Conolly becomes the "savage" Owen Jack. Jack, however, is an overstatement; the social manner of Bernard Shaw was somewhere between Conolly and Jack. Jack is perhaps a confession of how far overboard the young Shaw was going in his attempts to gain attention.

Jack's brutishness is not merely in social manner; it is also a physical fact. "A sort of Cyclop with a voice of bronze" (p. 22), Jack is short and thick-chested. His face, marked by smallpox, is extremely ugly. It is Adrian Herbert's opinion that "Nature does

not seem to have formed Mr. Jack for the pursuit of a fine art"
(p. 8). That smallpox must have been an afterthought for it is
a fact that during the writing of this novel in 1881 Shaw was
stricken with smallpox (despite childhood vaccination) and almost died of it. Pearson terms the experience "a humiliating ex-
posure of his mortality."[12] Shortly after the illness Shaw began
growing the Satanic red beard, possibly to cover the pockmarks.
In any case, the ugliness of Owen Jack contributes to his diaboli-
cal appearance. I agree with Nethercot that Jack is Shaw's first
real diabolonian.[13] He has a very wicked look that he often uses
to frighten people, especially servants, and when he is thwarted
by circumstances he shakes his fist at the sky (p. 41).

The effect of Jack's presence is to make the delicate souls of
conventional society feel their fragility. They fear Jack as a china
shop owner fears a bull, for Jack is a breaker of the thin cups and
saucers of social habit. Herbert warns Mary of "the injury that
can be done by the mere silent contact of coarse natures with fine
ones" (p. 32). Jack is to be treated as one would treat a dangerous criminal. He fulfills the definition of the outlaw by constantly disrupting the smooth workings of the social law. Mary
remarks that "Jack creates nothing but discord in real life, whatever he may do in music" (p. 130). But there is paradox here.
Jack is an outlaw in art as well as life. Herbert and the academicians rant about his "lawless composition" (p. 129) that is completely void of melody. Yet Madame Szczympliça insists that it
is full of melody. As for Jack's social note, the adolescent Charlie
gets along quite harmoniously with Jack. In short, here is Shaw's
first statement of the paradox of harmony and discord. The dis-
cordance of Jack's social note, as well as his musical note, is really
a new kind of harmony, which only the unaffected child and the
fellow genius can appreciate. It is really the others who are discordant with the new melody.

There is further paradox in that while the unbound Prome-
thean is a terror to those still bound by conventions, yet in his
unpredictable freedom lies most of his appeal. Though scandal-

12. Pearson, p. 58.
13. Arthur Nethercot, *Men and Supermen*, p. 60.

ized by him, society finds that it cannot do without him. " 'Society' found relief and excitement in the eccentric and often rude manner of the Welsh musician, and recognized his authority to behave as he pleased" (p. 174). In the character of Jack, Shaw had discovered the phenomenon of the privileged lunatic, and subsequently developed it in his own personality. He had learned how many people escape from their ordinary selves by vicariously identifying with a social buffoon, expressly tolerating him for that purpose.

The toleration is not unanimous, however. Lady Geraldine, for instance, "was a lady of strong common sense, resolutely intolerant of the eccentricities and affectations of artists. . . . Society, in her opinion, had one clear duty to Jack—to boycott him until he conformed to its reasonable usages" (p. 174). When Jack strongly agrees with the commonsensical advice he had overheard Lady Geraldine giving to Mary, she is much astonished: "Well, really! . . . Is this the newest species of artistic affectation, pray? It used to be priggishness, or loutishness, or exquisite sensibility. But now it seems to be outspoken common sense; and instead of being a relief, it is the most insufferable affectation of all" (p. 179). There seems to be no pleasing Lady Geraldine, but Jack is being lionized by nearly everyone else.

His partial acceptance by society, acceptance of his musical genius at least, betrays Jack into a weak desire for further acceptance. "Why have I less right to the common ties of social life than another man?" (p. 198). Upon his shocking Mary Sutherland by a proposal of marriage, she asks him if a true artist can really have any concern for marriage or money. He replies ironically: "No, of course not. Music is its own reward. Composers are not human; they can live on diminished sevenths, and be contented with a pianoforte for a wife, and a string quartette for a family. . . . I am a privileged mortal, without heart or pockets. When you wake up and clap your hands after the *coda* of Mr. Jack's symphony, you have ministered to all his wants, and can keep the rest to yourself, love, money, and all" (pp. 198–99). Dropping the irony, he says: "When I took to composing, I knew I was bringing my pigs to a bad market. But dont pretend to believe that a composer can satisfy either his appetite or his affections with music any more than a butcher or a baker can" (p. 198).

After such speeches from the heart, Mary wonders if she should sacrifice herself for the sake of Jack, but Jack reads in her face the repugnance she really feels. He speaks in a stirring voice: "I have committed my last folly. . . . Henceforth I shall devote myself to the only mistress I am fitted for, Music. . . . I have broken with the world now; and my mind is the clearer and the easier for it. . . . I hanker for a *wife*! . . . I grovel after *money*! What dog's appetites have this worldly crew infected me with! No matter: I am free: I am myself again. Back to thy holy garret, oh my soul!" (pp. 201–3). This speech has reminded critics of the final scene in *Candida*, where the poet Marchbanks turns his back on domestic comfort and strides out into the night, secure in the secret knowledge that genius does not need love.[14] It's difficult to know what to make of this, to decide whether Shaw is ridiculing Jack and Marchbanks or not. Jack's previous commonsense speech about the needs of the man being unfulfilled by the products of the artist sounds rather more Shavian, but the unpublished young Shaw, nearly friendless in great London, must have felt an equal necessity for extreme dedication to his art. Shaw may have felt the call to the "holy garret" sincere enough, yet simultaneously thought it ridiculous. "There are times when composing music seems to me to be a ridiculous thing in itself," says Jack (p. 149).

Although Jack is Shavian enough to occasionally see the absurdity in his rigid attitude of artistic probity, he cannot help assuming such extreme postures. He is violently intolerant of amateurs, and only fear of poverty can force him into "teaching female apes to scream, that they may be the better qualified for the marriage market" (p. 197). His is a one-man campaign against the abuses of music, especially his own. He is much given

14. For an account of the many scenes and characters that Shaw the playwright drew from the novels, see Stanley Weintraub's "The Embryo Playwright in Bernard Shaw's Early Novels," *The University of Texas Studies in Literature and Language*, pp. 327–55.

to stomping out of the theatre when the orchestra improperly executes the score. So extreme is his intolerance of artistic ineptitude that even Madame Szczympliça reproves him for insulting "those who are less fortunately gifted than he" (p. 145). But if Jack is such a monster of artistic propriety, it is because, in Shavian fashion, he feels a mystical connection between art and ethics. Jack refuses a bandmastership with the army on the grounds that he would not be "the hireling of professional homicides" (p. 100). Music and ethics are deeply involved with one another. There are two kinds of art, says Jack. "There is an art that is inspired by nothing but a passion for shamming . . ." and "there is an art which is inspired by a passion for beauty, but only in men who can never associate beauty with a lie. That is my art" (p. 330). Nethercot believes that "It is a bit of a surprise to hear Shaw's mouthpiece reiterating that beauty is truth and truth beauty, and that that is all men need to know about art. . . . It is pure art that commands his allegiances at this time—art untouched by any hint of didacticism or utility."[15] Now there are plenty of hints of didacticism in Shaw's novels, but Nethercot is right that Shaw's allegiance at this time is to Keatsian theory, if not always to Keatsian practice. This should not be surprising, as Shaw, even after adopting the didactic theory, insisted upon the unity of beauty and truth. He almost always took great pains to speak truth beautifully, or to express beauty truthfully. It is a tenet of the higher didacticism that nothing is more beautiful than truth when truth is beautifully told.

If Jack's artistic posture strikes us as absurd, we must understand it in the context of nineteenth-century estheticism. Jack's volatile artistic temperament seems to us a cliché, mechanical in its predictable unpredictability, but it was an expression of revolt against the even more mechanical cliché of a contemporary ideal, as represented by Adrian Herbert. Adrian explains Jack's deficiencies. Jack "has taken up an art as a trade, and knows nothing of the trials of a true artist's career. No doubts of himself; no aspirations to suggest them; nothing but a stubborn narrow self-sufficiency. I half envy him" (p. 109). Jack "is so far from

15. Nethercot, p. 139.

possessing the temperament of an artist, that his whole character, his way of living, and all his actions, are absolutely destructive of that atmosphere of melancholy grandeur in which great artists find their inspiration. His musical faculty, to my mind, is as extraordinary an accident as if it had occurred in a buffalo" (p. 157). And so the two clichés about the artistic temperament come head to head. It used to be that you could tell an artist by his Agonizing Doubts, Refined Manner, Delicate Sensibility, and Melancholy Disposition; nowadays "mere brute skill carries everything before it" (p. 296), and the true artist is marked by supreme confidence in his genius and a robust rejection of all the prescribed forms of behavior. A significant difference between the two kinds of artist is in the class pretensions of the former. When Jack enlisted a trombone-playing soldier found in a local tavern to accompany him in his composition, Adrian overhears the result and is very much affected by the music until he sees the maker of it, whereupon he despised "the whole art of music because a half-drunken soldier could so affect him by it" (p. 31).

After his marriage to Aurélie, Adrian disintegrates as an artist as he becomes the slave of his love. He perceives that "life is larger than any special craft" (p. 295). The surface irreverence of his wife has shown him "that earnestness of intention, and faith in the higher mission of art, are impotent to add an inch to his artistic capacity. They rather produce a mental stress fatal to all freedom of conception and execution" (pp. 295–96). Disillusioned, Adrian comes to see the very little importance of being earnest in matters of art, since genius is clearly an accident of nature that takes no account of class or sartorial suitability in forming an artist.

Much the same conclusion is arrived at on the female side of the question. The three major female characters—Aurélie Szczympliça, Madge Brailsford, and Mary Sutherland—represent three different levels of artistic ability. Aurélie, on the top level, is unmistakably a genius; Madge, on the second level, is a fine craftsman with moments of genius; Mary, "a woman of force and intelligence," cannot for all her high seriousness achieve anything beyond the amateur, though her intelligence makes her a

discerning critic of the work of others. Mary instinctively recognizes the weakness in Adrian's work, just as she feels the force of
genius in Jack's work.

Mary Sutherland, though, is a very puzzling character, puzzling because she takes up so much of the novel. A count would
surely show her having more lines and scenes than any other character. Woodbridge notes that she is the character "who is most
nearly central in the plot. . . . Such semblance of unity as the
novel has depends largely on her."[16] It is difficult to account for
Shaw's interest in her. As Woodbridge says, since she has "nothing bizarre about her, she is not a Shavian type. She is a serious,
high-minded girl, with some wit but not much fun in her, whose
chief virtue is perhaps her tolerant generosity."[17] Perhaps we can
account for her central position through the character of Jack.
Jack is such a rude, noisy, willful character that, for the sake of
consistency, Shaw could not readily use him for straightforward
comment on the happenings of the novel. Though limited by her
class prejudices, Mary's combination of quiet sense, honesty, and
"tolerant generosity" provide a kind of moral norm for the book
through which the other characters are reflected. Mary is something of an emergent New Woman, mildly scornful of conventional propriety and rather masculine in her walk and general
authority. She rules her father with an iron hand. It is against this
background of the mildly rebellious daughter of the upper class
that we are able to measure the rebellious character of Owen Jack
and Madge. It is against the background of her critical intelligence that we can measure the relative artistry of Jack, Herbert,
and the others. And it is against the background of her tolerant
generosity that we measure the intolerance of class prejudice. Perhaps this would have been a better novel if Jack had commanded
the center throughout. Certainly it would have been more spirited; but apparently Shaw felt the need of an ethical center which
Jack's brute behavior, overstating Shaw's case for the irrational,
could not supply. If Shaw had kept Jack in the center, I think
he would have become more like Conolly. It is significant that

16. Woodbridge, pp. 12–13.
17. *Ibid.*, p. 12.

Conolly is reintroduced in the final chapters and provides the rational voice on the question of "love among the artists" which Mary cannot supply herself since she is involved in it.

If Shaw had come to the end of rationalism by his third novel, he had not come to the end of Edward Conolly. Somehow one gets the feeling that the really dangerous man in this novel is not Owen Jack but Ned Conolly. He poses a far greater threat to society through his practical, economic subversion of conventional values than does Jack through his merely artistic rebelliousness. Jack's brutal aggressiveness is an important qualification of the Shavian hero, but Shaw comes back to Conolly because his practical concerns are closer to Shaw's own preoccupations at this time. The heroes of the final two novels will be more like Conolly than like Jack. Conolly's influence upon genteel society has been insidious. When invited out to Lady Geraldine's, he declares himself contentedly "at home" (p. 228). Lady Geraldine is secretly gratified at this and sensibly accepts cultured, rich tradespeople as an improvement over the old style of ladies and gentlemen. After all, she says, "who is a gentleman nowadays?" (p. 231).

On the question of marriage, Lady Geraldine is all for the practical Mr. Hoskyn (Hoskyn is Conolly without genius or culture). She counsels Mary that taking a husband is not "the same thing as engaging a gentleman to talk art criticism with" (p. 233). So much for Adrian Herbert. Mary has been her father's housekeeper too long to feel uncomfortable as the wife of a practical man like Hoskyn. And "a perfect husband is one who is perfectly comfortable to live with" (p. 232). For that reason, genius "is a positive disqualification. Geniuses are morbid, intolerant, easily offended, sleeplessly self-conscious men, who expect their wives to be angels with no further business in life than to pet and worship their husbands. . . . They are not comfortable men to live with" (p. 232). So much for Owen Jack. Conolly then explains to her why she should not marry a man like himself, a man who has achieved her ideal of a self-disciplined man. Giving an objective account of his marriage to Marian, Conolly explains how the model husband had led his wife "to believe that he would be as happy without her as with her. A man who is complete in himself needs no wife" (p. 237). So Hoskyn, who is far from being the complete man, and who indeed *needs* Mary to complement his cultural deficiencies, is the perfect mate for her. And that is the way it turns out, as symbolized by their offspring. Mary's baby is a "healthy and smiling" child, in contrast to the baby of Aurélie and Adrian, which always looks sad and old.

Aurélie Szczympliça is perhaps the most charming of Shaw's many astonishing female creations.[18] The Polish pianist is an elusive character, "as evasive as a bar from a Chopin mazourka."[19] She doesn't really fit any of the clichés about either women or geniuses, although Shaw undoubtedly meant for her to present the female side of the character of genius. She regrets her marriage to Adrian, as she finds it interfering with her art. To her, love is the most stupid thing in the world. To Adrian she confesses: "I cannot love. I can feel it in the music—in the romance —in the poetry; but in real life—it is impossible. I am fond . . . of the *bambino*, fond of you sometimes; but this is not love. . . . I see people and things too clearly to love. Ah well! I must content myself with the music. It is but a shadow. Perhaps it is as real as love is, after all" (p. 314). Aurélie has come to agree with Jack that "it is marriage that kills the heart and keeps it dead. Better starve the heart than overfeed it. Better still to feed it only on fine food, like music" (p. 329). Aurélie refuses to conform to the image that other people have of her. When Charlie tries to make a Candida of her by becoming infatuated with his poetic image of her, Aurélie irately tells him that he is very mistaken: "I am not what you think me to be. I am the very other things of it. I have the soul commercial within me" (p. 337). However poetic she looks, she is at one with the unpoetic-looking Jack in having the soul commercial within her and in seeing things too clearly to love. Once and for all, Shaw seems to be saying, artistic genius is not a matter of poetic appearance or noble intentions.

18. Robert Louis Stevenson, in a letter to William Archer, expressed his Victorian alarm at the masculinity of Shaw's females with, "I say, Archer, my God, what women!" (Henderson, p. 128).

19. James Huneker, "Bernard Shaw and Woman," *Harper's Bazaar*, p. 536.

Shaw repeats the lesson of the discrepancy between the innocent vision of a life of art with the hard-working reality of such
a life many times in the course of this and other novels. He de-
votes a long chapter to a detailed account of the rising career of
Madge Brailsford in its several stages, revealing, by the way, his
thorough knowledge of the stage years before he became a dramatist. At first Madge "ridiculed the notion that emotion had
anything to do with her art . . . the matter being merely one of
training" (p. 121). A love affair then opened her eyes to the
value of emotion, causing her to despise her "complete method."
She goes to the opposite extreme in declaring "that study and
training were useless, and that the true method was to cultivate
the heart and mind and let the acting take care of itself" (p. 121).
Later she achieves synthesis when she understands that "She had
had to exhaust the direct cultivation of her art before she could
begin the higher work of cultivating herself as the source of that
art" (p. 124). I think that statement of synthesis explains the
art of Bernard Shaw as well as any I have seen.

As Hesketh Pearson puts it, the novel has no catastrophe and
no ending, it just stops.[20] It stops with Aurélie's disillusioning of
Charlie, before her tour in America, which will leave Adrian
behind, and with Charlie's decision to take a job with Conolly
Electro-Motor Co. Just before this, in his only scene in Book II,
Owen Jack has disillusioned Madge about the possibility of romance. "Juliet must not fall in love with Friar Lawrence, even
when he is a great composer" (p. 330). Besides, he has no need
of special romance. "Romance comes out of everything for me.
Where do you suppose I get the supplies for my music? And
what passion there is in that!—what fire—what disregard of
conventionality! In the music, you understand: not in my everyday life" (p. 328).

Jack argues, in a manner that has become conventional, that
as his art has its source in the "heart," the heart must not be
killed by stuffing it with the food of love. The great artist is a
hungry man, great in art because hungry as a man. At least that
is what the hungry, unloved young Shaw had decided, momen-

20. Pearson, p. 58.

tarily. In his more extreme Shelleyan moments, Shaw was capable of believing that the body of the Superman could be fed with spiritual food, but in his saner, more Shavian moments, some of which occur even in this novel, he saw that the Superman to survive must get along on the world's terms ("Money is the root of all good," says John Tanner) and protested the tendency of society to make of him a Kafkaesque "hunger artist."

If *The Irrational Knot* went too far in the direction of rationalism, *Love Among the Artists* goes too far in the opposite direction of irrationalism. Doubtless the extreme thesis of *The Irrational Knot* made necessary the extreme antithesis of *Love Among the Artists*. The reintroduction of Conolly in the last part of the latter, however, suggests that Shaw had already sensed a need for synthesis before he had completely finished his statement of antithesis. Perhaps that is why he brought the novel to such a swift conclusion and proceeded to a fresh statement of synthesis in the next novel.

The Mind and Body of the Superman
(Cashel Byron's Profession)

*There are pugilists to whom the process of aiming
and estimating distance in hitting, of considering the
evidence as to what their opponent is going to do,
arriving at a conclusion, and devising and carrying
out effective counter-measures, is as instantaneous
and unconscious as the calculation of the born arith-
metician or the verbal expression of the born writer.
This is not more wonderful than the very complicated and deeply considered feats of breathing and
circulating the blood, which everybody does con-
tinually without thinking; but it is much rarer, and
so has a miraculous appearance.*

BERNARD SHAW
Preface to
Cashel Byron's Profession

The quotation above makes perfectly explicit Shaw's symbolism
of the mind and the body. Simultaneously as the body stands
for itself, it also stands for the largest and most important part
of the mind. The body refers both to itself as the fleshly reposi-
tory of biological drives, motives, appetites, and physical power,
and to itself as the embodiment of the unconscious mind. The
"rapid reasoning" of the mind finds its perfect symbol in the
rapid reasoning of the body, as both are swift, natural, unconscious, and marks of genius. The man who "thinks" with his
body, like Owen Jack the musician or Cashel Byron the pugilist,
can be as much of a genius and a visionary as the man who
thinks with his mind alone. Indeed Shaw's point is that the man
who thinks with his mind alone cannot be considered a genius
unless he uses the muscle of his brain in the same way that Cashel
Byron uses the muscle of his arm. Shaw came to see that the
trouble with conventional nineteenth-century rationalism was
that it assumed that the brain is exclusively a machine, and fur-

thermore a machine constantly at war with the "flesh," rather than the supersophisticated muscle or organ that it really is. The problem of *Cashel Byron's Profession*, then, is that of work-ing out a synthesis between the supposedly rational mind and the irrational body.

In constructing the plot of his fourth novel, Shaw seems to have made rare concessions to popular tastes, but an intelligent reading shows that the concessions were either superficial, or per-haps in the nature of a joke upon the popular press.[1] The story line is pure Horatio Alger, Local Boy Makes Good. The or-phaned hero, Cashel Byron, runs away from school at an early age, becomes boxing champion of England and the colonies in his young manhood, marries a wealthy heiress, and discovers himself to be of noble birth. He spends the remainder of his life fighting for noble causes as a member of Parliament, living as happily ever after as people are ever allowed to do at the end of a Shaw work. Were there nothing more to this novel than the bare plot suggests, we would be justified in dismissing the novel as unworthy of critical analysis.

But Shavian frivolity was always on the surface; beneath, in the depths of Shaw's didactic heart, was always a lesson for whoever wanted to go to school. And his being an inveterately autobiographical writer adds even greater weight to the apparent lightsomeness of this novel. Critics have been misled into believ-ing that the autobiographical element is missing in this novel by the fact that the hero is an uncultured pugilist of distinctly non-intellectual habits.[2] Other than the boxing, there seems to be

1. In the preface to *Cashel Byron's Profession*, p. xi, Shaw admitted that he tried to win the favor of publishers by making his novel conform, at least superficially, to what they expected of a novel: "In novel-writing there are two trustworthy dodges for capturing the public. One is to slaughter a child and pathosticate over its deathbed for a whole chapter. The other is to describe either a fight or a murder. There . . . lay the whole schoolboy secret of the book's little vogue. I had the old grievance of the author: people will admire him for the feats that any fool can achieve, and bear malice against him for boring them with better work."

2. "There is no autobiographical element in the story," says Wood-bridge, p. 15.

little that Shaw and Cashel Byron have in common.[3] The misunderstanding is caused by Shaw's trying something new. In the
other novels he had fixed the autobiographical element mostly
upon a single male person; but in this novel he experiments with
a dialectic. Besides being themselves, the hero and the heroine are
the body and the mind of Bernard Shaw, as the young man was
working out their relationship. Like the good Greek humanist
he was, his conclusion was the marriage of body and mind. Conventionally enough for the Victorian Age, Shaw made the mind
female and the body male. He would later reverse that, in Mil-
tonic fashion, in *Man and Superman.*

The mind of Shaw is represented by the character of Lydia
Carew. William Irvine, who doesn't like rationalists, says that
Shaw in creating Lydia "allowed that superlogical electrical inventor, Conolly, after nearly ruining one story, to don petticoats
and scramble into the principal role of another."[4] Allowing for
the physical, psychological, and social differences between male
and female, that's true enough, although in her occasional sen-

3. Besides being an avid boxing fan, Shaw "was for many years a very
passable boxer" (Irvine, p. 29).

4. Irvine, p. 30. On the subject of Lydia Carew, one ought to read
Shaw's remarks in "Mr. Bernard Shaw's Works of Fiction Reviewed by
Himself," p. 238: "Lydia is superhuman all through. On the high authority of William Morris (privately imparted) she is a 'prig-ess.' Other
critics, of a more rationalistic turn, revere her as one of the noblest creations of modern fiction. I have no doubt that the latter view is defensible;
but I must admit that, for a man of Morris's turn, her intellectual perfec-
tions are rather too obviously machine-made. If Babbage's calculator is
ever finished, I believe it will be found quite possible, by putting an extra
wheel or two in, to extend its uses to the manufacture of heroines of the
Lydia Carew type. Doubtless the superior mechanical accuracy of Lydia's
ratiocinative action is calculated to strike awe into the average super-
stitious bungler, just as the unfinished machine of Babbage strikes awe
into me. . . . *Of course I too, fall far short of Lydia Carew in the reasonableness of my private conduct.* Let me not deny . . . that a post-mortem
examination by a capable critical anatomist . . . will reveal the fact that
her inside is full of wheels and springs. At the same time it must be distinctly understood that this is no disparagement to her. There is nothing
one gets so tired of in fiction as what is called 'flesh and blood' " (italics
added).

tentiousness and priggishness she seems to retrogress beyond Conolly to Robert Smith.

Lydia's upbringing is suspiciously like John Stuart Mill's. Her father was a writer of books intellectual and cultural. Daughter and father spent much of their time traveling, sight-seeing, reading, and theorizing. By the time Lydia is twenty-five, she has a reputation for "vast learning and exquisite culture" (p. 24). At the novel's inception, her father has recently died and left her a wealthy woman, the heiress of a huge estate and Wiltstoken Castle, "a nondescript mixture of styles [Turkish, Moorish, Egyptian, and Italian Renaissance] in the worst possible taste" (p. 23). "All the rooms there were either domed, vaulted, gilded, galleried, three sided, six sided, anything except four sided: all in some way suggestive of the Arabian nights' entertainments . . ." (p. 180). The strange Eastern architecture and interior decorations exactly accorded with the lower-class idea of aristocratic splendor. Lydia found it all rather unbearable and did most of her work on the biography of her father outside the castle. She has managed, however, to impose some of her tastes upon the furnishings. "Everything was appropriately elegant; but nothing had been placed in the rooms for the sake of ornament alone. Miss Carew, judged by her domestic arrangements, was a utilitarian before everything" (p. 42).

The "dismal science" of utilitarianism accounts for much of Lydia's behavior. She is "interested by facts of any sort" and writes letters only when she has something factual and informative to say (pp. 109, 172). Echoing Conolly, she says, "Work is one of the necessaries of life" (p. 69). Among the many "manlike proceedings" that scandalize her friends is her capacity for business, including accounting. She has a manner of making people believe she is interested in them (p. 174), but her interest in people seems to be an extension of her interest in facts. She has the statistician's habit of treating people as facts useful in the inductive process of reasoning. And, like later Shavian heroes, she has a realistic appreciation of human motive, never deluding herself, for instance, about the motives of friendship. "Absolutely disinterested friends I do not seek, as I should only

find them among idiots or somnambulists. As to those whose interests are base, they do not know how to conceal their motives
from me" (p. 109). Furthermore, far from despising her wealth,
Lydia pragmatically sets "great store by the esteem my riches
command" (p. 109).

Lydia is equally utilitarian in her attitude toward art. When
her politician cousin, Lucian Webber, warns another that
Lydia's "pet caprice is to affect a distaste for art, to which she is
passionately devoted; and for literature, in which she is pro-
foundly read," Lydia replies, "Cousin Lucian . . . should you
ever be cut off from your politics, and disappointed in your
ambition, you will have an opportunity of living upon art and
literature. Then I shall respect your opinion of their satisfac-
toriness as a staff of life. As yet you have only tried them as a
sauce" (p. 49). If one cannot live by bread alone, the Shavian
always reminds us that survival for all but the most dedicated is
even less likely on art alone.

Recalling the esthetic regard of Smith, Conolly, and Jack for
the railroad, it is not surprising to hear Lydia's opinion that
"Clapham Junction is one of the prettiest places about London"
(p. 79). Her companion, Alice Goff, "thought that all artistic
people looked on junctions and railway lines as blots on the landscape," a thought that inspires Lydia to poetic rebuttal:

> Some of them do . . . but they are not the artists of our gen-
> eration; and those who take up their cry are no better than
> parrots. . . . The locomotive is one of the wonders of modern
> childhood. Children crowd upon a bridge to see the train
> pass. . . . Little boys strut along the streets puffing and whis-
> tling in imitation of the engine. . . . Besides . . . a train is a
> beautiful thing. Its pure white fleece of steam harmonizes
> with every variety of landscape. And its sound! Have you
> ever stood on a sea coast skirted by a railway, and listened
> as the train came into hearing in the far distance? At first
> it can hardly be distinguished from the noise of the sea; then
> you recognize it by its variation: one moment smothered
> in a deep cutting, and the next sent echoing from some hill-

side. Sometimes it runs smoothly for many minutes, and then breaks suddenly into a rhythmic clatter, always chang- ing in distance and intensity. When it comes near, you should get into a tunnel, and stand there whilst it passes. I did that once; and it was like the last page of an overture by Beethoven, thunderingly impetuous. . . . Abuse of the rail- way from a pastoral point of view is obsolete. There are millions of grown persons in England to whom the far sound of the train is as pleasantly suggestive as the piping of a blackbird. [pp. 79–80]

This seems to be the definitive word on the new relationship be- tween art and the machine. Machines are not to be automatically disqualified as unesthetic.

Lydia is equally Millite in her politics. Democratically, she believes that "a native distinction and grace of manner [can be found] as often among actors, gipsies, and peasants, as among ladies and gentlemen" (p. 55). Yet as these native talents pro- vide us with a natural aristocracy, Lydia is democratic only to get at the real aristocracy. Lydia's democracy was not of the coonskin variety any more than was Shaw's or Mill's. If she is a leveler, her method is to "level up, not down." Although she keeps servants, she allows them the run of her library in the hope that they will better themselves. She would like everyone to be as clever as she is.

As befits a progressive Victorian intellectual, Lydia is also in- ternationalist: "In the course of my reading I have come upon denunciations of every race and pursuit under the sun. Very respectable and well-informed men have held that Jews, Irish- men, Christians, atheists, lawyers, doctors, politicians, actors, artists, flesh-eaters, and spirit-drinkers, are all of necessity de- graded beings. Such statements can be easily proved by taking a black sheep from each flock and holding him up as the type" (p. 128). She will have nothing to do with theories of racial, national, religious, or professional superiority, for superiority is purely an accident of nature, concerning individuals alone.

With beliefs like these, Lydia finds herself pretty much alone in class-conscious England. The Tory Lucian argues that their marriage would be compatible enough because her opinions "are not represented by any political party in England; and therefore they are practically ineffective, and could not clash with [his]." Lydia replies that "such a party might be formed a week after our marriage—will, I think, be formed a long time before our deaths. In that case I fear that our difference of opinion would become a very personal matter" (p. 112). (As a matter of fact, the Fabian Society is less than a year away.)

One is made to wonder, however, if Lydia's lack of political commitment is due to the absence of a party to which she can give her allegiance or to the intellectual habit of non-commitment. Her idea of truth is not particularly compatible with political action. She believes that "reticence is always an error" (p. 110). Truth must always come out. The trouble is that she has a rationalist's rather than a pragmatist's idea of truth. That truth is relative and a matter of consequences she will not admit. She is sure that the consequences of lying are always the same: "The one convicton she had brought out of her reading was that the concealment of a truth, with its resultant false beliefs, must produce mischief, even though the beginning of that mischief might be as inconceivable as the end. She made no distinction between the subtlest philosophical sophism and the vulgarest lie" (p. 188).

Yet when the police are after Cashel Byron for illegal boxing, Lydia hides Cashel and lies to the police. She even causes her footman, Bashville, to lie. During it all she "felt as if the guilt of the deception was wrenching some fibre in her heart from its natural order" (p. 185). After the police have left, she declares that "the very foundations of my life are loosened," and bids Cashel never to darken her door again. She drops Cashel not so much because of any crime he had committed but because he was an imposter (she was unaware of his prize-fighting) and had forced her to lie in his behalf.

The evil of Cashel's capture was measureable, the evil of any lie beyond all measure. She felt none the less assured of that evil because she could not foresee one bad consequence likely to ensue from what she had done. Her misgivings pressed heavily upon her; for her father, a determined scep' tic, had left her destitute of the consolations which theology has for the wrongdoer. It was plainly her duty to send for the policeman and clear up the deception she had practised on him. But this she could not do. Her will, in spite of her reason, acted in the opposite direction. And in this paralysis of her moral power she saw the evil of the lie beginning. She had given it birth; and Nature would not permit her to strangle the monster. [pp. 188–89]

Obviously Lydia Carew, with her rationalist's regard for the police, is a long way from becoming a political revolutionary, although she is making some progress toward that end. Later, for the first time, she tells a very small social lie for the sake of sparing another's feelings, and fancies "that she was beginning to take a hardened delight in lying" (p. 202). Still, it is Cashel and not Lydia who ultimately goes into politics, for Lydia is of the type who can never sacrifice without discomfort her notions of absolute truth to the narrow demands of a political creed.

We should not misunderstand Lydia as merely a scholarly recluse, bumbling, inept, and timid in all matters requiring action. In her own sphere of social action she is quite competent. Although she lives without ceremony, "whatever Lydia did was done so that it seemed the right thing to do" (p. 54). Her little bourgeois companion, Alice Goff, wonders at Lydia's "secret of always doing the right thing at the right moment, even when defying precedent" (p. 170). But there is a significant change from the manner of Jack, Conolly, and even Smith in the way she feels about her mastery of real propriety. She agrees with Mary Sutherland (now Mrs. Hoskyn) that there is a difference between good manners and conventional manners, but, she says, "one can hardly call others to account for one's own subjective ideas" (p. 96). This is quite a switch from the proselyting spirit being developed in the other novels, and I don't think Shaw is approving it. Rather, this is one more example of the deficiencies of the high and dry intellect, uninspired by the evangelical body. Further, there is a contradiction in her behavior in that while she is willing to trust her social instincts, she is not willing to trust the impulse to lie in Cashel's behalf. The difference is that while social instinct is almost purely physical, the impulse to lie is cerebral in origin and thus she does not trust it.

Lydia understands quite well the deficiencies of her rationalism, thus her motive for marrying Byron. She declares herself "sick to death of the morbid introspection and ignorant self-consciousness of poets, novelists, and their like" (p. 221). "If one could only find an educated man who had never read a book" (p. 79). Such outbursts of anti-intellectualism are understandable as reactions against the scholar's life, which Lydia, like many another scholar, is willing to undersell. Believing herself "not good at intuitions, womanly or otherwise" (p. 111), she thought herself a "well-taught plodder" in comparison to the genius of Mrs. Byron (p. 155). (Byron's mother is a famous actress.)

Lydia is confirmed in her self-devaluation by a letter left to her by her father to be read after his death. During their lives the relationship of father to daughter had been one of scholar to amanuensis or clerk, but in the letter the scholar struggles to express his heart. He begins by acknowledging that he belongs "to the great company of disappointed men" (p. 27). Lest Lydia develop a sense of injustice at the apparently selfish use he made of her, he wishes to justify himself. He explains the egotistical character of her mother, whom he divorced after six unbearable years of marriage. He then explains that although he made use of Lydia without scruple, he never did so without regard to her own advantage, as he never imposed a task of no educational value on her. In time, the promise of his young daughter brought pleasure to a life that he otherwise thought barren and wasteful. He began to be concerned about her future, as "the world has not yet provided a place and a sphere of action for well-instructed women" (p. 29). However, he does not counsel accommodation with the world: "In my younger days, when the companionship of my fellows was a necessity to me, I tried to set aside my cul-

ture; relax my principles; and acquire common tastes, in order
to fit myself for the society of the only men within my reach; for,
if I had to live among bears, I had rather be a bear than a man.
The effort made me more miserable than any other mistake I
have ever made. It was lonely to be myself; but not to be myself
was death in life. Take warning, Lydia: do not be tempted to
accommodate yourself to the world by moral suicide" (p. 29).
As for choosing a husband, his counsel is heavy with a sense of
the futility of advising anyone in matters of the heart. He has
only one prejudice: "Beware of men who have read more than
they have worked, or who love to read better than to work. Do
not forget that where the man is always at home, the woman is
never happy. . . . Self-satisfied workmen who have learnt their
business well, whether they be chancellors of the exchequer or
farmers, I recommend to you as, on the whole, the most tolerable
class of men I have met" (p. 30). Such is the advice of a man who
calls himself "an educated stone," "an overcivilized man" (p.
30). Much later, when Lydia is wavering over the question of
marriage, she comes across a poem that her father had marked
as a favorite:

What would I give for a heart of flesh to warm me through
Instead of this heart of stone ice-cold whatever I do!
Hard and cold and small, of all hearts the worst of all.

Lydia recoils at this, and, after long thought, speaks to herself:
"If such a doubt as that haunted my father, it will haunt me, unless I settle what is to be my heart's business now and forever.
If it be possible for a child of mine to escape this curse, it must
inherit its immunity from its father, and not from me—from
the man of impulse who never thinks, and not from the rationaliz-
ing woman, who cannot help thinking. Be it so" (p. 204).
    "The man of impulse who never thinks" is Cashel Byron. As
proof that he never thinks, "There isnt a more cheerful lad in
existence" (p. 203). Lydia describes him as "a man who had
never been guilty of self-analysis in his life—who complained
when he was annoyed, and exulted when he was glad, like a

child and unlike a modern man—who was honest and brave, strong and beautiful" (p. 222). When she first comes across him training in the woods behind Wiltstoken, she feels as though "she had disturbed an antique god in his sylvan haunt" (p. 36). He is like a beautiful Greek statue who delights her by coming alive. (In contrast, Byron thinks her a ghost, or an angel, and her house a fairyland.) Byron as sylvan god is reminiscent of the innocent Donatello in Hawthorne's *The Marble Faun,* except that Byron does not lose his essential innocence. He remains a child, and Lydia treats him as the greatest of her children.

If he does not lose his innocence, Byron does lose his "home." Rather he never really seems to have had a home. He is another disconnected young man who abides, against his will, in the boarding house–orphanage that is the Moncrief House school for sons of gentlemen. He does have one live parent, and no other Shaw hero in these five novels can make that statement, but that parent might as well be dead. His actress mother, Adelaide Gisborne, alienated him as a child by her changeable, hot-tempered treatment, causing him to reserve his affection for the servants. Quite early in his life she farmed him out to a boys' school, visiting him only on rare occasions. When the master of the school summons her for an interview regarding the deport-ment of her son, she makes no effort to understand Cashel's side of the argument and agrees with the master that her son is a bad boy. After this interview, Cashel exclaims, "I hate my mother" (p. 8) and runs way from the school, scaling the wall in the best prison break fashion. He stows away on a ship bound for Australia, becomes a sailor for a while, then meets Ned Skene and his wife (Skene being a former boxing champion now operat-ing a gymnasium) who become his adopted parents. From then on he speaks of Mrs. Skene as his real mother, even after Lydia engineers a partial reconciliation between Cashel and Mrs. Byron. In short order Skene makes a champion of Cashel and together they return to England.

To be a boxing champion had not been Cashel's first ambition. His original ambition—to go into the army—had been quite respectable. But when his escape from Moncrief House makes him a sort of escaped convict, he decided "to go to sea, so that if his affairs became desperate, he could at least turn pirate, and achieve eminence in that profession by adding a chivalrous humanity to the ruder virtues for which it is already famous" (p. 10). Here again is the chivalric rogue, whose involuntary outlawry prevents him from taking his rightful place among the respectable professions of society. Like the profession of the later Mrs. Warren (and the profession of the later Fabian propagandist named Shaw), the professions of piratry and prizefighting are outside the sphere of acceptable occupations. Yet the "chivalrous humanity" and essential gentlemanliness of Cashel creates the paradox of the chivalric outlaw. Lydia comes to the realization that, after all, "Ivanhoe was a prizefighter." This in turn makes her wonder if "some romancer of the twenty-fourth century will hunt out the exploits of my husband, and present him to the world as a sort of English nineteenth century Cid, with all the glory of antiquity upon his deeds" (p. 219).

The point about Cashel's basic superiority to the society which ostracizes him is made in two different scenes. First, there is the scene in which as a test of their natures Cashel deliberately insults Lucian Webber and invites Lucian to take a poke at him. Lucian is a relatively puny intellectual who lives in terror of physical violence of any kind, yet "his point of honor, learnt at an English public school, was essentially the same as the prizefighter's" (p. 217). Ultimately fear of dishonor overwhelms the fear of physical injury, causing Lucian to take a wild, harmless swing at Cashel, after which Cashel congratulates him for showing pluck and cheerfully bids him good day. But Lucian is sickened by the revelation of his inner self; he sees "no escape from his inner knowledge that he had been driven by fear and hatred into a paroxysm of wrath against a man to whom he should have set an example of dignified control" (p. 218). Lydia is ecstatically happy when she discovers that Cashel did not retaliate. (Cashel is one Byron who, unlike the poet, fights only for cash, thus his name.) She had wondered whether the brutality of Cashel was evidence of his deepest nature or merely professional. Now she knows. "He has beaten you on your own ground,

Lucian. It is you who are the prizefighter at heart; and you grudge him his superiority in the very art you condemn him for professing" (p. 224).

The other scene that points up Cashel's moral superiority occurs near the end of the novel. After having been shamed by causing Lydia to lie in his behalf, Cashel gives himself up to the police and stands trial. The result is an imposture of a trial. The establishment of boxing, like that of prostitution, is, however illegal, generally winked at because of its secret popularity. The defense of the miscreants is brilliantly sophistic, carried on by "an eminent Queen's counsellor, whose spirits rose as he felt the truth change and fade whilst he rearranged its attendant circumstances" (p. 228). When the whole defense was presented, Cashel "was awestruck, and stared at his advocate as he half feared that the earth would gape and swallow such a reckless perverter of known facts" (p. 228). The judge himself had handled the gloves in his youth, and he along with "the more respectable persons in court, became extraordinarily grave, as Englishmen will when their sense of moral responsibility is roused on behalf of some glaring imposture" (p. 228). Cashel and his opponent are found guilty of a common assault, given a suspended sentence and a promise of fine if they fight again in the next twelve months. As Cashel leaves the trial a free man, he exclaims, "By Jingo . . . if we didnt fight fairer than that in the ring, we'd be disqualified in the first round. It's the first cross I ever was mixed up in; and I hope it will be the last" (p. 229). Byron had complained to Lydia earlier, when she accused him of being antisocial in his profession, that it was unfair for him to "be put out of decent society when fellows that do far worse than I are let in. . . . If all these damned dog-bakers and soldiers and pigeon-shooters and fox-hunters and the rest of them, are made welcome here, why am I shut out like a brute beast?" (pp. 135–36).

It is a question that Lydia is very hard put to answer. For all her advanced opinions and philosophic radicalism, Lydia still shares some of the prejudices of her class, one of them being that prizefighters are not gentlemen. She is confused by the natural gentility she senses in Cashel and the brutality he displays in the

ring, not understanding that the brutality is that of Ivanhoe, not
Attila the Hun. Upon being invited to one of Mrs. Hoskyn's at
homes as a celebrity, Cashel rather incongruously harangues his
drawing room audience for five solid pages on the necessity of
Ivanhoe's getting an "executive power."

> We have been told that if we want to civilize our neighbors,
> we must do it mainly by the example of our own lives, by
> each becoming a living illustration of the highest culture we
> know. But what I want to ask is, how is anybody to know
> that youre an illustration of culture? . . . You want an
> executive power: thats what you want. Suppose you
> walked along the street and saw a man beating a woman,
> and setting a bad example to the roughs. Well, you would
> be bound to set a good example to them; and, if youre men,
> youd like to save the woman; but you couldnt do it by
> merely living; for that would be setting the bad example of
> passing on and leaving the poor creature to be beaten. What
> is it you need to know, then, so as to be able to act up to
> your ideas? Why, you want to know how to hit him, when
> to hit him, and where to hit him; and then you want the
> nerve to go in and do it. . . . thats whats wanted worse than
> sitting down and thinking how good you are. . . . Dont you
> see? You want executive power to set an example. If you
> leave all that to the roughs, it's their example that will
> spread, and not yours. [p. 87]

Later Cashel will have a chance to test this philosophy when
Lydia brazenly walks through one of the poorer sections of London and is molested by a tough. As Cashel just happens to be
passing by, he comes to her rescue. Although Cashel is not eager
to fight, the tough is, until he discovers the identity of the champion and chooses the better part of valor. That's executive power,
and if it sounds familiar it's because John F. Kennedy said much
the same thing about politics a few years ago. Politics, he said in
effect, is a dirty business that naturally attracts dirty people and
naturally repels decent people, and that's all the more reason

why good men should get executive power by going into politics. Lydia Carew, the intellectual without a party, and almost without a conviction, feels frustrated by the "incommunicability of ideas," and, while she intellectually understands that to communicate even the noblest idea "one must take one's gloves off" (p. 62), she is temperamentally disinclined to enter the arena herself. After their marriage, it is Cashel who fights for her ideas in Parliament. It is the ignoble body that must go out to do battle in the name of the noble mind.[5]

Ivanhoe's executive power makes him nearly unbeatable, but Shaw admits a set of circumstances that can defeat even the genius with executive power. Byron twice engages a savage by the name of William Paradise. The first exhibition is stopped when Paradise tears off his gloves, rushes Cashel before he can do likewise, and gnaws on Cashel's shoulder with his teeth.[6] The second affair was the bare-knuckle bout broken up by the police. In both cases Cashel had beaten Paradise to a bloody pulp, but Paradise refused to fall. Shaw explains his meaning in the preface: "there is a well-known way of defeating the pugilistic genius. There are hard-fisted, hard-hitting men in the world, who will, with the callousness of a ship's figurehead, and almost with its helplessness in defence, take all the hammering that genius can give them, and, when genius can hammer no more from mere

5. It is sometimes difficult to tell whether Shaw's characters are intentionally contradictory in their characterizations for ironic purposes or whether the contradictions arise from Shaw's natural, instinctive artistry getting the better of his conscious theorizing. To put it another way, because Shaw always put more of himself into his characters than the plan perhaps called for, his characters turn out to be human beings as well as symbols, rather than just symbols. Just as Conolly is more than rationalist, Owen Jack more than willful genius, so Cashel Byron is not merely the unthinking Greek body he was probably supposed to be. He turns out to be a rather thoughtful young man, just as Lydia is far more active than the inert body she was probably meant to represent.

6. About this bloody affair, described in vivid detail, Shaw once wrote, "Out of the savagery of my imagination I wrote the scene; and out of the savagery of your tastes you delight in it" ("Mr. Bernard Shaw's Works of Fiction Reviewed by Himself," p. 236).

exhaustion, give it back its blows with interest and vanquish it" (p. xviii).

Although Shaw was temperamentally disinclined to think much about defeat, here is an early awareness of the tragic potential in the career of genius, the awareness that not all the moral genius in the world, fully equipped with executive power, can subdue the brute in creation.

The point is that the brute must be fought, and it can be fought only on its own terms. When Cashel engages Paradise, Shaw writes that in Cashel "there was no chivalry and no mercy . . ." (p. 165). When Ivanhoe is fighting the Black Knight, he is foolish to abide by the chivalric code. Lydia struggles to understand this. Byron's "perpetual fighting metaphor" indicates to her his attachment "to the modern doctrine of a struggle for existence . . . life as a continual combat." Byron agrees: "Just so. What is life but a fight? The curs forfeit or get beaten; the rogues sell the fight and lose the confidence of their backers; the game ones, and the clever ones, win the stakes, and have to hand over the lion's share of them to the moneyed loafers that have stood the expenses; and luck plays the devil with them all in turn. Thats not the way they describe life in books; but thats what it is" (pp. 99–100).

Keeping in mind that pugilism is a metaphor for the fighting spirit and executive power that Shaw felt necessary to the noble cause, this view of life as a strife of wills is central to the Shavian philosophy; but we must carefully distinguish it from the pseudo-Darwinian. If Shaw is arguing for the survival of the fittest, he does not define the fittest as merely the physically strongest. By "fit" he means fit for human society. Furthermore as the strife can bring out the best in one and make life more meaningful and more clearly defined, people should be encouraged to participate.[7] At least this is the view of the young Shaw who was about

7. In his "The Conflict of Wills in Shaw's Tragicomedy," *Modern Drama*, pp. 414–15, Norbert F. O'Donnell writes, "Ultimately, the worst thing which can happen to an individual in the strife at the psychological center of Shavian drama . . . is to be 'intimidated' or 'discouraged' by another human will. It is in this way that one experiences the humiliation of

to abandon his role as spectator and become an amateur Fabian, with every intention of rising to the level of the top professional.

There is another paradox here. With Shaw there is always another paradox. Our Shavian hero is an Ivanhoe struggling to make the world a better place, but only because fighting is natural to him. According to Byron: "All this struggling and striving to make the world better is a great mistake; not because it isnt a good thing to improve the world if you know how to do it, but because striving and struggling is the worst way you could set about doing anything. It gives a man a bad style and weakens him. It shews that he dont believe in himself much" (p. 91). Here Byron is repeating the realization that came to Adrian Herbert at the end of *Love Among the Artists*. "Nothing can be what you might call artistically done," says Byron, "if it's done with an effort. . . . The more effort you make, the less effect you produce. . . . Ease and strength, effort and weakness, go together" (pp. 91–93). For example Byron points to a painting by Adrian of St. George and the dragon. St. George is in conventional fighting posture, but Byron argues that "one touch of a child's finger would upset him . . . because he's all strain and stretch . . ." (pp. 92–93). More graphically Byron illustrates his point by gently placing his hand against the breast of Lucian, who has pugnaciously challenged his opinions, whereupon Lucian "instantly reeled back and dropped into the chair" (p. 94). This lesson is an important qualification of the strife of wills: it seems there is an art to striving, and the quickest way to fall short of one's goal is to force one's art. In short, if one isn't a natural born world-betterer, one should find something else to do. Shaw's chief objection to the "do-gooder" was that he tries too hard.

The lesson is universal, it seems. Alice Goff, Lydia's hired companion, finds it to be true in social matters. When Lydia first

becoming merely an object in another's world, merely a means to another's personal ends. . . . This discouragement obviously involves an overpowering fear, a sense of total inability to grasp the purposes of the other, and a disintegration of the will. In a world in which humanity consists of an ability to participate as an equal in psychological strife, it is the basic evil."

engaged her, Alice was insufferably bourgeois. She believed that
good manners were measured by their stiffness and formality.
Proper behavior was the very opposite of natural behavior, and
therefore something to be struggled for. Propriety seemed to consist largely in being as uncomfortable as possible. Alice's salvation is that she is a robust young country girl who longs "for
swift motion and violent exercise," and under the tutelage and
example of Lydia she comes to understand that what natural
grace she possesses in her mere physical presence is superior to
and more trustworthy than the artificial poses of conventional
etiquette that she has relied upon. She comes to understand that
these poses are prescribed by etiquette because the bourgeois is
insecure in his social manner, not trusting himself to act cor-
rectly by behaving naturally. By the end of the book, Alice finds
the great commercial middle class to be "all a huge caricature of
herself—a society ashamed of itself, afraid to be itself, suspecting
other people of being itself and pretending to despise them for
it, and so stifling and starving itself . . ." (p. 171). Alice now understands that instead of being well mannered she was merely
self-conscious. She sees the distinction between "the most mannered [and] the best mannered." So it is "true that effort de-
feated itself—in personal behaviour . . ." (p. 171) as well as in
boxing.

The lesson of *Cashel Byron's Profession* is chiefly a physical
one. Figuratively speaking, it is a much-needed boxing lesson that
Shaw is, first of all, giving to himself, and, secondly, to all who
share his awareness of evil and his impotence to fight it. Far from
being a frivolous book, this novel is rather profound in theme
and philosophy, if not in character and action. One of its chief
lessons—that effort defeats itself—is being purveyed these days
by J. D. Salinger, who unnecessarily went to Zen to get it.

Shaw's novel moves along on at least three levels, one of
which is clearly autobiographical. First there is the objective
story of the local boy who makes good. Then there is the general
and rather explicitly symbolic story of the clash between the
Millite mind and the Darwinian body then occurring in Victorian society, with the marriage of that mind and that body

being Shaw's solution. And, finally, there is the autobiographical confession of the synthesis between mind and body that Shaw was working out in his own being.

On the first level Shaw ends the story with a joke. Lydia had decided to marry Byron as "a plain proposition in eugenics." "I believe in the doctrine of heredity; and as my body is frail and my brain morbidly active, I think my impulse towards a man strong in body and untroubled in mind a trustworthy one" (p. 223). But Lydia discovers that "heredity is not so simple a mat-ter as her father's generation supposed" (p. 231). She bears four precocious children, all of them smarter than their father; "the boys disappointed her by turning out almost pure Carew, with-out the slightest athletic aptitude, whilst the girls were impetu-ously Byronic . . ." (p. 232). So much for eugenics.

On the second level Shaw suggests that the marriage of the Millite mind and the Darwinian body is, like most partnerships, an unequal affair, for the body is really quite helpless, a child at heart, and relies heavily upon the mind for judgment, moral strength, and information. There's no doubt that Lydia controls Cashel, and that all the trouble of the family is hers. But there is one benefit for her. Taking care of such a troublesome family leaves her little time to think about herself. The morbidity of the Millite mind is healthfully transformed by preoccupation with the strategic matters of directing a family and a Parliamentary career.

Lastly, the autobiography of Shavian being concludes on a triumphant note. The novel ends with a sense of wholeness, as if in preparation for a mighty endeavor that will require a whole man. Shaw has finished with the measuring of his mind and the training of his body; now he is ready for battle. At that he lacks is a religious impulse to set him going, and in the next novel Karl Marx will provide that.

Bernard Shaw's Profession
(An Unsocial Socialist)

A little past midnight . . . I was turning from Pic-
cadilly into Bond Street, when a lady of the pave-
ment, out of luck that evening so far, confided to me
that the last bus for Brompton had passed, and that
she should be grateful to any gentleman who would
give her a lift in a hansom. My old-fashioned Irish
gallantry had not then been worn off by age and
England; besides, I was touched by the similarity
of our trades and predicaments.

BERNARD SHAW
Preface to
The Irrational Knot

With my egotism, my charlatanry, my tongue, and
my habit of having my own way, I am fit for no call-
ing but that of saviour of mankind.

SIDNEY TREFUSIS
in *An Unsocial Socialist*

By the time Shaw had embarked on his fifth novel, he had come
to a far better understanding of himself. He had come to see
that the difference between himself and most others was a difference in degree, not in kind. He possessed the same sort of mind
as other people, except that his mind was a little further developed that most. This special quality of mind made him unusual,
all right, but it did not make him the monster from outer space
he sometimes felt himself to be. This understood, he could then
better see the humor in the way certain people acted as though
he *were* a monster, and thus he learned to play his presumed
monstrosity as a deliberate joke upon both others and himself.
Far from being a handicap, his monstrosity provided him with a
wonderful device to instruct people in the difference between

the real and the apparently real. Further, this ironic acceptance of his role made him considerably more at peace with himself, and prevented him from becoming the sort of fanatic whose scourging of the world always ends in the world's striking back with matyrdom for the fanatic.

Perhaps there are two basic kinds of pure fanaticism, that of the detached intellectual who in scorn isolates himself from the world (see Joyce's James Duffy), and that of the Savanarola type of crusader who attempts by brutally coercive methods to impose his obsession upon society. In either case, the mark of the pure fanatic is the willingness to kill, to sacrifice life, for the sake of his ideal. In the first case, the obsessed is willing to kill himself by living a living death for the sake of remaining undefiled by the corruption of common humanity; in the second case, the obsessed is willing to kill others for the sake of removing the source of corruption. Although there is a bit of the fanatic in all of us, most of us are able to release our lesser fanaticisms in relatively harmless ways. For the extraordinary man, however, such as Bernard Shaw, the man who is "fit for no calling but that of saviour of mankind," the possibility of pure fanaticism is always present and seldom harmless.

Shaw's five novels reveal that the question of fanaticism was a very real issue to him. Characters like Robert Smith, Owen Jack, Ned Conolly, and Lydia Carew express an early tendency on the part of the lonely, introverted young Shaw to withdraw in contempt from the world of vain flesh, a tendency redeemed only by his social instincts and the Shavian habits of common sense and good humor. There can be no doubt that, as the novels indicate, the struggle to extrovert himself was long and arduous. Though we with our hindsight may declare the outcome inevitable, to Shaw himself at the time the struggle must have seemed very uncertain. If we find it difficult to imagine a Shaw residing all his life in an ivory tower, the young Shaw who was devoted to Shelley would not have found it so difficult. Yet one feels throughout the reading of these novels that the sort of fanaticism that will provide the greatest threat to Shaw is not the suicidal fanaticism of the ivory tower intellectual, but the murderous fanaticism of Savanarola, "fit for no calling but that of saviour of mankind." We see tendencies in the Shavian hero that, once he has found his faith, could lead to extremes of intolerance.[1] To see the truth of this we need look only at the history of this century to see the path of blood followed by the other disciples of the very holy and blessed St. Marx. It is thus with a sense of relief that we discover in *An Unsocial Socialist* a Shavian hero, fully extroverted and religiously motivated by Karl Marx, whose blend of common sense and good humor qualifies his revolution-ary zeal just enough to avoid fanaticism. The hero, Sidney Trefusis, luckily sees himself as a clown prophet rather than a fanatic, whose task is to convert through Socratic education and logical persuasion rather than through bloody purgation of the body politic.

Of his fifth novel Shaw once said, with characteristic thor-oughness, "People who will read An Unsocial Socialist will read anything"; he thereby relieved himself of the burden of defending it. Defending it is indeed a burden. There is first of all the discrepancy between Shaw's professed intentions and the seemingly different results. In writing the novel he had resolved "to give up mere character sketching and the construction of models for improved types of individual, and at once to produce a novel which should be a gigantic grapple with the whole social problem. But, alas! at twenty-seven one does not know every-thing! When I had finished two chapters of this enterprise— chapters of colossal length, but containing the merest preliminary matter—I broke down in sheer ignorance and incapacity."[2] So *An Unsocial Socialist* is merely the first two chapters of an un-finished work. Perhaps taking Shaw's cue, critics have dismissed

1. Consider Robert Smith's statement: "I would not give a half-penny for the faith of a votary who would not cut off the whole human race if it differed from him" (*Immaturity*, p. 269). The explanation for this and other such quotations is that when Shaw spoke like a pure fanatic, he was employing the literary device of overstatement. The words of fanaticism spoken by a Shaw would doubtless sound differently from the same words spoken by a Savanarola.

2. Quoted in Henderson, p. 106.

the novel for precisely being no more than "the merest preliminary matter." Henderson calls it "a brutal burlesque, full of mad
irresponsibility and cheap levity."[3] Weintraub says that in writing it "the gaily paradoxical Shaw had over-reached himself,
attempting to erect his ponderous economic edifice on a founda-
tion of whipped cream."[4] Among its earlier readers, the Macmillan critic declared it "a clever trifle" and hoped that Shaw
would try something "more substantial."[5]

In reply to Macmillan, Shaw shot off a letter protesting the
charge of trifling: "Your reader, I fear, thought the book not
serious—perhaps because it was not dull. If so, he was an Eng-
lishman. . . . You must admit that when one deals with two large
questions in a novel, and throws in an epitome of modern Ger-
man Socialism as set forth by Marx as a makeweight, it is rather
startling to be met with an implied accusation of triviality."[6]
If the older Shaw thought that the novel was no more than the
merest preliminary matter, the young Shaw who did the writing
of the novel thought that he had created something quite substantial, however preliminary.

The problem is further complicated by a criticism of Woodbridge's which insists that "The book does not square with this
account of its origin. It contains indeed a considerable amount
of socialist preaching, but it is also a good story, with a plot as
unified and symmetrically developed as any which Shaw had
produced, and with some of his best-drawn characters. The fact
seems to be that in spite of himself he was still more interested in
the characters and what happened to them than he was in his
socialist theories."[7] That the characters, created for the sake of
demonstrating an economic theory, nevertheless come to life
and exist independently of their intended economic allegory may
account for the sense of frivolity that many critics detect. The
characters all seem rather startled by the heavy Marxian intru-

3. Henderson, p. 107.
4. Weintraub, "Introduction" to *An Unfinished Novel*, p. 12.
5. Quoted in Henderson, pp. 116–17.
6. *Ibid.*, p. 117.
7. Woodbridge, p. 18.

sion, and the economic situations in which the author throws them in order to demonstrate his theory seem so ludicrous that the only response to this Shavian Marxism can be laughter. So wildly disconnected seem theme and character that readers of such ponderous tomes as Marx's *Capital* and Henry George's *Progress and Poverty,* or even the Fabian tracts, must by comparison think Shaw's work a Peacockian *jeu d'esprit.* Now Shaw's characters, and many of the situations in which they find themselves, are indeed frivolous; but that is the point. The comic contrast is between the gay, irresponsible world of English society and the dark crime of social mismanagement of which it is guilty. The lighter and gayer the spirit of the English rich, the heavier and sadder the crime of unbrotherliness it is committing. The point of the book is precisely in the contrast between upperclass levity and the economic burden of the poor. Shaw's first response to this contrast is typically not one of burning indignation and frothing at the mouth. He is so deliriously happy at having it brought to his attention that he can think of nothing but bringing it to the attention of others as the great joke that it really is. It is fitting that the most socialistic of Shaw's novels should also be his gayest. As Irvine puts it, "Gaiety is his natural artistic medium. Moreover, he had found a new faith. He was exuberantly happy in a dazzling new certainty."[8]

8. Irvine, p. 31. Of relevance here is the commentary of Claude T. Bissell in "The Novels of Bernard Shaw," *The University of Toronto Quarterly,* pp. 50–51: "His novels are about the wealthy and the aristocratic; they show an almost morbid consciousness of economic distinctions; and yet he has no consistent point of view toward the society he depicts. He seems to waver between an inclination to idealize a class to which, he is convinced, he rightfully belongs, and a feeling of resentment that wealth and social prestige should so often be accompanied by a cultural development immeasurably inferior to his own. . . . What Shaw needed, then, both to clarify his own personal problems and to give strength and direction to the works of his imagination was a plausible and consistent critical attitude toward the economic structure of society. . . . Much of the value of socialism consists for him in the solution it offers for his personal problems. Now that he has a coherent theory, he finds that he can adjust himself with ease to the present economic structure of society while, at the same time, he looks forward to the ultimate communist Utopia of absolute equality. . . . Shaw's

To illustrate his certainty Shaw wrote a novel in which the most frivolous situations and characters are shown to have heavy, economic significance. The "whipped cream" of social manner is weighty with hidden economic motive. Shaw did not need to go into the manufacturing jungles of Manchester or Liverpool to make his economic point; that would have been too easy and too obvious. So utterly confident was he of the Marxian point of view that he dared to show its relevance in the places and situations farthest from Manchester—in a country school for girls and on the rural estate of landed gentility. You would expect to find Marx in a Manchester factory, but what the devil is he doing in the drawing room? In short, the critical confusion has been caused by another Shavian paradox—the relevance of Marx is most substantial where the life of England is most insubstantial.

William Archer tells the story of the first time he met Shaw. In the reading room of the British Museum, Shaw was encountered reading almost simultaneously from Marx's *Capital* and Wagner's *Tristan and Isolde*.[9] There in a nutshell is Bernard Shaw, and *An Unsocial Socialist* is essentially an expansion of that scene. Much of the comedy of the book comes from the juxtaposition of romance and economics, and the dizzying rapidity with which the hero moves from one to the other.

The opening scene is an unlikely one for a novel purporting

---

romantic imagination and his power of comic invention, far from being stifled by his immersion in the dismal science, have been gloriously released. . . . Shaw found in *Das Kapital* . . . a new and exhilarating explanation of the mystery of experience, and a wealth of fascinating ideas that provided both the inspiration and the materials for literary expression. In the vision of a communist Utopia, Shaw found an ideal that would satisfy his romantic yearnings. In the socialist demonstration of the glaring incongruities underlying the economic structure of society, he found just the material he needed for the exercise of his comic genius. Henceforth he could be a social critic and a moralist without fear of falling into dullness and didacticism; for he now saw that the final truth of a matter reveals itself only to the artist-philosopher who combines a passionate imagination with an exquisite levity of mind."

9. Rattray, p. 43.

to be a Marxian analysis of a rotting capitalist society. It begins with three young schoolgirls sliding down the banister at Alton College, Lyvern. They are Agatha Wylie, a spirited nonconformist whose talents of mimicry, ventriloquism, and candor keep her forever in trouble with the authorities; Jane Carpenter, a stout, practical, simple-minded girl whose inevitable comment is "I never heard of such a thing"; and Gertrude Lindsay, a haughty, self-conscious girl who insists a bit too much upon her good breeding, the mark of the underbred. The hero, Sidney Trefusis, manages to find time to romance all three, and ultimately marries their ringleader, Agatha.

Before that, the millionaire Trefusis busily works his Marxist wiles among the English peasantry, making converts and generally laying the groundwork for the revolution. He has just run away from his new bride, Henrietta Jansenius, and assumed the disguise of Jeffrey Smilash, humble peasant, who abides in an equally humble cottage near Alton College. As Henrietta's father, a wealthy merchant, is also the guardian of Agatha Wylie, Trefusis does not long remain undetected in his disguise. When Agatha is threatened with expulsion, Mr. and Mrs. Jansenius, accompanied by their newly deserted daughter, Henrietta, visit Alton College to plead for Agatha's reinstatement. Trefusis-Smilash has by this time made the acquaintance of Agatha and has been hired to do odd jobs around the college. Not long after arriving, Henrietta recognizes Smilash as her recently lost husband and faints in his arms. While Agatha, the only observer of this scene, scurries for help, Trefusis grabs Henrietta and runs for cover. After eluding a posse, Trefusis at great length explains to his lovely young wife why he had to desert her. Briefly, Marx and marriage do not mix. Henrietta is simply too distracting. He somehow talks her into returning to London without giving away his disguise to the others, and is eventually captured by the police; but a telegram from Henrietta in London assuring her safety argues his acquittal.

Agatha meanwhile has been conjuring up a romance about the mysterious Smilash. In her presence he frankly drops his yokel accent and speaks as the well-bred son of an aristocrat of trade that he is, a technique that causes Agatha to imagine all sorts of heroism. The romance is heightened when one stormy night Trefusis bangs on the door of Alton College and pleads for hospitality for a peasant and his family whose flimsy house was destroyed in the storm. Such heroism causes Agatha to fall adolescently in love. Smilash encourages her with some pretty words, calling her his "golden idol." This is harmless flirtation so far, but trouble ensues when Agatha writes a letter to Henrietta confessing her secret lover. As Henrietta knows who Smilash is, in a rage she immediately embarks for Lyvern to confront her husband with the criminal letter. Trefusis explains the harmlessness of his philandering, protests his undying love, and packs her off back to London.

As this all occurs on the coldest day of the year, Henrietta comes down with pneumonia and shortly dies. Trefusis returns to London for the funeral, but behaves in a most scandalous way. He quarrels with Jansenius over his hypocrisy and over the matter of a tombstone epitaph. In order to make an economic point, Trefusis searches for a mason who will construct a tombstone at a fair price. When he refuses to attend the funeral, he quickly develops the reputation of a beast, exactly what you would expect of a socialist. Agatha meanwhile has learned the truth, and in her horror and disillusionment withdraws into herself. After several seasons in London society she remains unmarried.

Although this novel is not divided into two books, it certainly should be, for here we have a shift of scene and a lapse of a few years. As Irvine describes the change, "Sylvan fairy tale becomes Marxist-Ibsenite social drama. . . . Shavian intellectual drama is obviously struggling to be born."[10] Most of the action takes place either on the estate of Sir Charles Brandon, baronet husband of the former Miss Jane Carpenter, or at the family mansion of Trefusis, called Sallust's House. Jane had developed into a handsome, ample woman, and Sir Charles married her under the delusion that her beauty and sensuous charms promised great sympathy with his own artistic aspirations. Jane is still stout in mind, however, and she quickly disillusions him as

10. Irvine, p. 32.

to her sexual and intellectual talents, at which Sir Charles tried "to drown his domestic troubles in art criticism" (p. 187).

The Brandons first encounter Trefusis when they find him leading a pack of laborers in a march across one of Brandon's fields, claiming it as a right-a-way. Jane "never heard of such a thing," but she is so susceptible to Trefusis' flirtations that she invites him to visit her. A bit later she also invites Agatha and Gertrude ostensibly for a class reunion, but really to rescue them from a life of maidenhood. The rest of the novel is concerned alternately with the evangelistic attempt by Trefusis to convert Sir Charles and his poet neighbor, Chichester Erskine, to socialism and with the involved philanderings of Trefusis among the ladies. Gertrude mistakes his intentions and plans suicide when she learns that he has proposed to Agatha, but Trefusis sweet-talks her into marrying Erskine, who all along has been harboring a tragic love for her. The novel ends with an ironic letter to the author from the *real* Sidney Trefusis, protesting that Shaw has misrepresented him as a heartless brute, but otherwise congratulating Shaw for his talent and regretting that he has no better employment for it than the writing of novels.[11]

The Sidney Trefusis of the novel seems to be aware of his parentage only because of its economic significance. He has inherited from his dead parents a considerable wealth, and has developed what now might be called the "Rockefeller syndrome." Like many another son of a rich man, he has a sense of guilt about the way in which the money was collected. His father "was a shrewd, energetic, and ambitious Manchester man, who understood an exchange of any sort as a transaction by which

11. Shaw's original title was *The Heartless Man.* Trefusis explains why in his letter to Shaw, pp. 254–55: "In noveldom woman still sets the moral standard, and to her the males, who are in full revolt against the acceptance of the infatuation of a pair of lovers as the highest manifestation of the social instinct, and against the restriction of the affections within the narrow circle of blood relationship, and of the political sympathies within frontiers, are to her what she calls heartless brutes . . . that, indeed, is exactly what I am, judged by the fictitious and feminine standard of morality. Hence some critics have been able plausibly to pretend to take the book as a satire on Socialism."

one man should lose and the other gain. He made it his object to make as many exchanges as possible, and to be always the gaining party in them" (p. 68). As a cotton manufacturer the elder Trefusis was responsible for the involuntary slavery of many wretched Englishmen, and now his son is left with the awful burden of a wealth he did not earn, "whilst the children of the men who made that wealth are slaving as their fathers slaved, or starving, or in the workhouse, or on the streets, or the deuce knows where" (p. 71).

The guilt is further compounded on his mother's side of the family, landed gentility. His mother's father had inherited considerable land which at first was settled by a fairly prosperous race of peasants, who paid him enough rent "to satisfy his large wants and their own narrow needs without working themselves to death" (p. 73). But his grandfather was a shrewd man. "He perceived that cows and sheep produced more money by their meat and wool than peasants by their husbandry. So he cleared the estate. . . . he drove the peasants from their homes" (p. 73). If anything, this is more wicked than what his father did, for his grandfather was born free and wealthy and could at least have lived and let live. His father, on the other hand, "had to choose between being a slave himself and enslaving others. He chose the latter, and as he was applauded and made much of for succeeding, who dare blame him? Not I. Besides, he did something to destroy the anarchy that enabled him to plunder society with impunity. He furnished me, its enemy, with the powerful weapon of a large fortune. Thus our system of organizing industry sometimes hatches the eggs from which its destroyers break" (p. 204).

The destroyers of capitalism are in such a minority, however, that they have first to build an engine of destruction—namely, a party of revolutionaries. Candidates for such a party are, according to Marxian theory, to be found among the exploited proletariat—thus Jeffrey Smilash. The pretext for the disguise is that Trefusis is hiding from his wife, but there is no reason why some other disguise would not have accomplished the same purpose, or even why a disguise is needed. Trefusis becomes

Smilash really because, in Shavian fashion, he has decided to play the economic fool to the madness of King Capitalism, a strategy that is not recommended in Marx.

Trefusis explains that he chose the name "Smilash" because he thought it gave a pleasant impression: it is "a compound of the words smile and eyelash. A smile suggests good humour; eyelashes soften the expression and are the only features that never blemish a face. Hence Smilash is a sound that should cheer and propitiate. Yet it exasperates. It is really very odd that it should have that effect, unless it is that it raises expectations which I am unable to satisfy" (p. 104). The name exasperates because while it suggests genial servility Trefusis the ironist protests too much his peasant humility. He aggravates the ladies and gentlemen by constantly stressing his inferiority through the use of clichés about the poor current in drawing rooms.

Smilash is deliberately reckless with the truth, for he is "of the lower orders, and therefore not a man of my word" (p. 35). He confesses to one of the Alton College teachers that he is a "natural born liar—always was. I know that it must appear dreadful to you that never told a lie, and dont hardly know what a lie is, belonging as you do to a class where none is ever told. But common people like me tells lies just as a duck swims" (p. 97). When hired to do a menial job, Smilash advises his employer: "I am honest when well watched . . ." (p. 39). When a local person protests that Smilash not be paid too much for a job because "it would only set him drinking," Smilash humbly agrees and argues that a lesser wage will keep him drunk until Sunday morning, which is all he desires until religion can take over. After all he is a common man, who "understands next to nothing," and since "words dont come natural to him," he can expect nothing more than the other dumb brutes of creation (pp. 39–40). As for the accusation by a neighboring farm boy that Smilash had been seen kissing Henrietta, Smilash effectively refutes it by reminding the police that "a lady . . . dont know what a kiss means" (p. 60), as physical stuff like that is practiced only by the lower classes. And of course the poor's indulgence in sex is directly responsible for their poverty, in the form of mouths to feed, so they've no one to blame but themselves. "Reverend Mr Malthus's health!" toasts Smilash (p. 90).

The poor have gotten themselves a bad character, and Smilash humbly agrees that it is largely a result of their lack of thrift. After rolling the lawn at Alton College for a few pence, he announces that he's going to "put up all this money in a little wooden savings bank I have at home, and keep it to spend when sickness or old age shall . . . lay their 'ands upon me" (p. 39). But when he uses some of Sidney Trefusis' saved money to improve the dilapidated peasant's cottage he has rented to go with his disguise, the landlord warns him that the rent will be raised, as "a tenant could not reasonably expect to have a pretty, rain-tight dwelling-house for the same money as a hardly habitable ruin" (p. 82). Struck by the truth of this, Smilash later chides the rector of Alton College for "flying in the face of the law of supply and demand" by overpaying him "threppence." "If you keep payin at this rate, there'll be a rush of laborers to the college, and competition'll soon bring you down from a shilling to sixpence, let alone ninepence. Thats the way wages go down and death rates goes up, worse luck for the likes of hus, as has to sell ourselves like pigs in the market" (p. 64). The Smilash sarcasm is beginning to show through bitterly here, which contributes to his acquiring a bad character. He is warned to mend his ways if he wants to get a better character. Smilash replies: "I am grateful to your noble ladyship. May your ladyship's goodness sew up the hole which is in the pocket where I carry my character, and which has caused me to lose it so frequent. It's a bad place for men to keep their characters in; but such is the fashion. And so hurray for the glorious nineteenth century!" (pp. 40–41).

Later Trefusis momentarily abandons his disguise to speak directly to Henrietta about the clichés they have been brainwashed with. "At Cambridge they taught me that [my father's] profits were the reward of abstinence—the abstinence which enabled him to save. That quieted my conscience until I began to wonder why one man should make another pay him for exercising one of the virtues" (p. 71). Beyond that was the question of what his father abstained from: "The workmen

abstained from meat, drink, fresh air, good clothes, decent lodging, holidays, money, the society of their families, and pretty
nearly everything that makes life worth living. . . . Yet no one
rewarded them for their abstinence. The reward came to my
father, who abstained from none of these things, but indulged
in them all to his heart's content" (p. 71). The only thing his
father abstained from more and more as he grew richer and richer
was work. As for his father's argument that his fortune was the
reward for "his risks, his calculations, his anxieties, and the jour-
neys he had to make at all seasons and at all hours," Trefusis
came to realize that this was an argument that would better fit
a highway robber (p. 72).

Trefusis is a kind of advanced Shelley who sees that the masks
of anarchy have shifted from the faces of kings to the faces of
capitalists. He has no use whatsoever for the old style Liberalism,
as represented by the poet Erskine, author of *The Patriot Mar-
tyrs*. Erskine is eager to show Trefusis that he is just as revolutionary as Trefusis: "Is it not absurd to hear a nation boasting
of its freedom and tolerating a king? . . . I admire a man that kills
a king. You will agree with me there, Trefusis, won't you?"
Trefusis certainly does not agree: "A king nowadays is only a
dummy put up to draw your fire off the real oppressors of
society, and the fraction of his salary that he can spend as he
likes is usually far too small for his risk, his trouble, and the condition of personal slavery to which he is reduced. What private
man in England is worse off than the constitutional monarch"
(p. 199). He then goes on to detail the trials and tribulations of
being a modern king. Fifty years later Shaw would expand this
paragraph into a play entitled *The Apple Cart*, in which King
Magnus gets his way with his cabinet by threatening to abdicate
and run for office. At the time Shaw was accused of turning
Tory in his old age, but this novel proves that his contempt for
the old style Liberalism was there from the beginning.

Erskine also provides Trefusis the occasion for debunking
artistic affectation. Erskine believes "that the sole refiner of
human nature is fine art," whereas Trefusis believes "that the
sole refiner of art is human nature. Art rises when men rise, and

grovels when men grovel" (p. 165). Trefusis heatedly denounces "the tyranny of brain force" by which less clever men are en-slaved, the artist being "the worst of all." "No men are greater sticklers for the arbitrary dominion of genius and talent than your artists" (p. 74). "[An artist] wants to be fed as if his stomach needed more food than ordinary stomachs, which it does not. . . . He talks of the higher quality of his work, as if the higher quality were of his own making . . . as if, in short, the fellow were a god, as canting brain-worshippers have for years past been assuring him he is. Artists are the high priests of the modern Moloch. Nine out of ten of them are diseased creatures, just sane enough to trade on their own neuroses" (pp. 74–75). Bernard Shaw was never more medieval than in his belief that genius was a gift that as Trefusis says, "costs its possessor noth-ing; that it was the inheritance of the whole race incidentally vested in a single individual; and that if the individual employed his monopoly of it to extort money from others, he deserved nothing better than hanging." Trefusis exclaims that artists were foolish "in fancying themselves a priestly caste when they were obviously only the parasites and favored slaves of the moneyed classes" (p. 135). Here is proof that Shaw was a share-the-wealther before there was anything like Fabian policy. Excep-tional gifts, whether they be gifts for writing novels or gifts for making money, should not, in the Socialist state, be rewarded by exceptional salaries.

Trefusis illustrates his contempt for the merely artistic by his neglect of Sallust's House. When Erskine and Sir Charles visit him for a lecture on Socialism, they are scandalized by the dis-repair the old, ornate mansion is in. It seems Trefusis has con-tributed to the normal decay by using the statuary for target practice. To the horror of his visitors, he takes out a pistol and decapitates a statue of Hebe.[12] He further startles them by de-claring photography the art form of the future. In photography "the drawing counts for nothing, the thought and judgment

12. In his "Introduction" to An Unfinished Novel, p. 12, Weintraub describes Trefusis as a combination of Sidney Webb, Bernard Shaw, and Annie Oakley.

count for everything; whereas in the etching and daubing processes, where great manual skill is needed to produce anything
that the eye can endure, the execution counts for more than the
thought . . ." (p. 159). In Trefusis' own photographic collection
is proof of the superiority of photography over painting. He converts Sir Charles to Socialism, at least temporarily, by over-
whelming him with seemingly matter-of-fact photographs of
working class conditions, the effect being heightened by a contrast with photographs of his father's immaculate stables full
of well-fed horses. Another collection is devoted to pairs of iden-
tical faces, one of which belongs to the nobility, the other to the
peasantry, thereby illustrating "the fact that Nature, even when
perverted by generations of famine fever, ignores the distinctions
we set up between men" (p. 205). A third collection contrasts
the noble faces of "Nihilists, Anarchists, Communards," etc.,
with the coarse, vapid faces of European royalty, thereby illustrating "the natural inequality of man, and the failure of our
artificial inequality to correspond with it" (p. 206). Sir Charles
is much impressed by the thoughtful art of Trefusis' photography, but the conversion is not clinched until he is apprised that
Mr. Donovan Brown, the famous artist, is also a Socialist. Donovan Brown is obviously William Morris, and for Shaw the symbol of the regeneration of art through political commitment.

Previously Erskine had called upon Trefusis for his opinion of
the future of the arts, and Trefusis responds with a vision of the
future that anticipates *Back to Methuselah*.

Photography perfected in its recently discovered power of
reproducing color as well as form! Historical pictures replaced by photographs of *tableaux vivants* formed and arranged by trained actors and artists, and used chiefly for
the instruction of children! Nine-tenths of painting as we
understand it at present extinguished by the competition
of these photographs, and the remaining tenth only holding
its own against them by dint of extraordinary excellence!
Our mistuned and unplayable organs and pianofortes replaced by harmonious instruments, as manageable as barrel

organs! Works of fiction superseded by interesting company and conversation, and made obsolete by the human
mind outgrowing the childishness that delights in the tales
told by grown-up children such as novelists and their like!
An end to the silly confusion, under the one name of Art,
of the tomfoolery and make-believe of our play hours with
the higher methods of teaching men to know themselves!
Every artist an amateur, and a consequent return to the
healthy old disposition to look on every man who makes art
a means of money-making as a vagabond not to be entertained as an equal by honest men! [pp. 160–61]

It is easy to explain this as a young novelist's reply to the Victorian art establishment that would not let him publish, or even
to his recent conversion to the new pragmatic politics of action
that has small use for pure art, but Shaw returned in his sixties
to the notion that all works of art are no more than dolls for
children. Doubtless here he is having a little joke at his present
state of being unpublished, but he also really meant it. In the
short run Shaw was as much the Artist-with-a-capital-A as the
"high priests of the Modern Moloch" denounced by Trefusis,
but in the long run he envisioned the ultimate disappearance of
art from the list of man's serious occupations. Whenever Shaw
exaggerates or deflates the importance of the artists, it is relative
to the short run or the long run.

Trefusis combines the visionary quality of the Shavian futurist
with a sometimes serious, sometimes comic involvement in the
present. After a long dissertation on the future of the arts or
the future of England under capitalism, he can abruptly turn to
the practical work of political conversion or to the frivolous
play of flirtation. In the latter case, he has a way of making
females think that they are his favorite. In regard to women,
Trefusis curses himself for being unable to "act like a rational
creature for five consecutive minutes" (p. 98). Women, brought
up on the idea that the only interest a man can have in woman
involves matrimony, are often misled by his trifling. "He had no
conscientious scruples in his love-making, because he was unac-

customed to consider himself as likely to inspire love in women"
(p. 239). More to the point is his love of a holiday. Trefusis'
"natural amativeness" is heightened by the sternly ascetic work
of the political revolutionary, so that holidays are essential to his
health. Trefusis tells Henrietta that he has left her because "I
have too much Manchester cotton in my constitution for long
idylls. . . . the first condition of work with me is your absence.
When you are with me, I can do nothing but make love to you.
You bewitch me . . ." (p. 77). But the separation is not to be
permanent, for he will occasionally return to her for a holiday.

So far this idea of the holiday is part of a permanent Shavian
attitude. Caesar will trifle for a moment with Cleopatra, just
as King Magnus will enjoy a romp with Orinthia. But in the first
flush of his conversion to the new economics, Shaw allows his
obsession to turn even this harmless bit of frivolity into a didactic
occasion. His objection to monogamy is that it is monopolistic.
And after the death of Henrietta, he makes all his flirtations
occasions for lectures on Socialism: "If you want to make a cause
grow, instruct every woman you meet in it. She is or will one
day be a wife, and will contradict her husband with scraps of
your arguments. A squabble will follow. The son will listen, and
will be set thinking if he be capable of thought. And so the mind
of the people gets leavened" (pp. 215–16). Further, he is
genuinely shocked when Gertrude Lindsay mistakes his philanderings for a serious proposal because, as far as he is concerned,
his making love to her was only a means of liberating her from
her false pride. He believes that she has good instincts which
only need instruction to cause her to throw off the bondage of
"convention, laws, and lies" that fence her round (p. 192). His
attentions are to make her see that the formal and false "Miss
Lindsay" is the bitterest foe of the natural "Gertrude," in that
the aversions of the conventional Miss Lindsay are forever con-
tradicted by the natural sympathies of Gertrude. Miss Lindsay
looks with disapproval upon "Bolshevists," but Gertrude is
powerfully attracted to Sidney Trefusis. In this she should trust
Gertrude. "I used to flirt with women," says the reformed Tre-

fusis, "now I lecture them, and abhor a man-flirt worse than I do a woman one" (p. 216).

Thus the distinction between Trefusis' first and second marriages is made on the basis of his attitude toward "romance" as strictly a holiday thing. The marriage to Henrietta was a horrible mistake because it was supported only by romance; the marriage to Agatha has a better chance because it is grounded in reality. Agatha succeeds with Trefusis because she is instructed by the outcome of her first, teen-age romance with him. Both had believed in the grand passion of the other, but knew that they felt nothing of the sort themselves. "That is the basis of the religion of love," Trefusis explains, "of which poets are the high-priests. Each worshipper knows that his own love is either a transient passion or a sham copied from his favorite poem; but he believes honestly in the love of others for him. . . . Is it not a silly world . . ." (p. 114). Of the women he knows, Agatha is "the only one not quite a fool" (p. 224). He decides to marry her upon the sudden realization that he "was made to carry a house on [his] shoulders" (p. 225). The proposal is more like Ned Conolly's than the early Trefusis'. They will spend their honeymoon at a Socialist conference in Geneva. She has one month to prepare the wedding.

We should not be surprised to find exaggeration and obsession in this novel. It is the work of a young man just rescued from the vacuum of Victorian nihilism, and it is only natural that he would be enthusiastic about his new economic vision. He is seeing the world differently, and not the smallest detail escapes his new economic vision. Yet never does his obsession become pure fanaticism, for his lively sense of the comic feeds on such fanaticism. Although as a Marxian revolutionary he knows the seriousness of the economic motive, as a comic novelist he knows the absurdity of the economic obsession.[13] Trefusis likes orchids because "a plant that can subsist on a scrap of board is an instance of natural econ[omy]" (p. 167). Absolute proof that it

13. There is one brief reference in this novel, p. 221, to the fact that Sidney Trefusis too has written some novels. Agatha speaks to Trefusis: "This is one of your clever novels. I wish the characters would not talk so much."

is the novel of a young man drunk on a conviction after a long abstinence is found in the letter from the real Trefusis to Shaw, complaining that the novel has been taken as a satire on socialism. Shaw was well aware of his over-indulgence, and could not resist a joke at the expense of his own tipsiness.

Even more outrageous is the joke that the later Shaw of the preface has at the expense of his younger self. The Shaw of 1930 declares that "The contemplated fiction is now fact. My unsocial socialist has come to life as a Bolshevist; and my catastrophe has actually occurred in Communist Russia. The opinions of the fictitious Trefusis anticipated those of the real Lenin" (p. v). But while there is a superficial resemblance between Trefusis and Lenin, their differences go deeper. Both have been called Machiavellian in their ethics, but Trefusis inherits from Robert Smith and the other Shaw heroes an aristocratic sense of propriety that is anything but Leninistic in its concern for the right way of doing things. When Trefusis violates the conventional code of truth-telling by going back on his promise to Erskine that he would not take the same train Gertrude is on, he is still not violating his own sense of propriety. He has misled Gertrude to the point that she may ruin her life, so he feels obligated to restore her by selling the marriage to Erskine. Fancy Lenin feeling any such obligation or performing any such task. The deception of Erskine was a harmless way to prevent him from ruining Trefusis' campaign in Erskine's own behalf—hardly a Machiavellian ploy.

Shaw seems to have rejected several other Marxist-Leninist attitudes and principles right from the beginning. Trefusis talks in campaign style about a revolution, but his methods are strictly pre-Fabian. He is a permeator, permeation being an evolutionary rather than a revolutionary method. Through the processes of argument and debate, the body politic is to gradually change its mind until it becomes something quite different in character. Bleeding of the body politic is to be kept to a minimum. According to Trefusis, "Socialism is often misunderstood by its least intelligent supporters and opponents to mean simply unrestrained indulgence of our natural propensity to heave bricks at respectable persons" (p. 79). Trefusis is also quite unconventional in his refusal to adopt the Marxian melodrama. According to the formula, his father should be a villain, but rather Trefusis congratulates him for avoiding the common lot of slavery and bringing order out of chaos. Furthermore, he does not romanticize the working classes, never failing to see them as individuals. When one of the laborers apologizes to Sir Charles for the demonstration, Trefusis calls him "a grovelling famine-broken slave" (p. 148). He will go "As gently as you please with any man that is a freeman at heart . . . but slaves must be driven, and this fellow is a slave to the marrow" (p. 149).

As for the slaves employed in his inherited Manchester factories, Trefusis is not about to set them free, for if he did they would simply become the slaves of some other factory owner undoubtedly less interested in their ultimate welfare. Worse yet, by freeing his wage-slaves, Trefusis would himself become a slave and lose the opportunity his money affords to carry on the work of reform. If the old commandment was, "Give all that ye have to the poor and follow me," the new commandment is, "Keep all that you have and work for the socialist state," for the poor will ultimately benefit more from that than from private charity. People who misunderstood socialism liked to accuse the wealthy Shaw of the 1920's and 1930's of not practicing what he preached, as if socialism were a private ethic that the individual can practice in isolation. Shaw apparently understood from the beginning, *when he was yet a very poor young man,* that wealth to do any lasting good must be invested in economic reform, not diffused by transient charity. When Erskine chides Trefusis for not selling all and giving to the poor, Trefusis replies:

A man cannot be a Christian in this country. I have tried it and found it impossible both in law and in fact. I am a capitalist and a landholder. I have . . . shares . . . and a great trouble they are to me. But these shares do not represent wealth actually in existence; they are a mortgage on the labor of unborn generations of laborers, who must work to keep me and mine in idleness and luxury. If I sold them,

would the mortgages be cancelled and the unborn generations released from its thrall? No. It would only pass into
the hands of some other capitalist, and the working class
would be no better off for my self-sacrifice. Sir Charles cannot obey the command of Christ; I defy him to do it. Let
him give his land for a public park; only the richer classes
will have leisure to enjoy it. Plant it at the very doors of the
poor, so that they may at least breathe its air, and it will
raise the value of the neighboring houses and drive the poor
away. Let him endow a school for the poor, like Eton or
Christ's Hospital, and the rich will take it for their own
children. . . . Sir Charles does not want to minister to poverty, but to abolish it. No matter how much you give to the
poor, everything except a bare subsistence wage will be
taken from them again by force. All talk of practising Christianity, or even bare justice, is at present mere waste of
words. [pp. 212–13]

Because a man cannot be a Christian in modern society, Trefusis finds that it is easy enough to be a Christ. He says, "With
my egotism, my charlatanry, my tongue, and my habit of having
my own way, I am fit for no calling but that of saviour of mankind . . ." (p. 104). The trouble is that mankind doesn't have
much use for saviours, except to crucify them and invoke their
name in vain. "The British workmen showed their sense of my
efforts to emancipate them by accusing me of making a good
thing out of the Association for my own pocket, and by mobbing
and stoning me twice" (p. 206). And then comes the distinctly
Fabian touch—"I now help them only when they shew some
disposition to help themselves. I occupy myself partly in working
out a scheme for the reorganization of industry, and partly in
attacking my own class . . ." (p. 206). Yet always the attack on
his own class was that of the clown prophet. There are perhaps
more differences than similarities between the characters of Jesus
and Bernard Shaw, but no difference is more significant than the
attitude toward martyrdom. Shaw's strong sense of anti-climax
(one might almost say "anti-martyrdom") was directly respon-

sible for his long life. After scarifying the Pharisees in a very Christ-like manner he would always relieve the tension with a joke, thereby winning acceptance rather than crucifixion.[14]

Quite the fashion in modern criticism is the theme of "mask" and "face." "The man and the mask" approach implies a "real" face behind a "false" mask, the mask merely serving a public function which the face is too sensitive to endure or too earnest to handle. Shaw criticism is full of this sort of apology for the "real" Shaw—the shy, gentle, gracious hermit of Ayot St. Lawrence. Archibald Henderson assures us that the real Shaw of his infrequent visits was nothing like the imaginary creature of common fame. Shaw himself chimed in with a debunking of G.B.S., claiming him to be a fantasy of journalism. And the epigraph of this chapter declares the clown character of his public performances to be "a fantastic character" deliberately created for the purpose of making himself "fit and apt for dealing with men." Now there is much truth to all this, but it is rather misleading and partly fallacious in its psychology.

Recent literature of the Salinger variety abounds with "phonies," people caught "playing the role," the implication in some Salinger criticism being that role-playing is psychologically dishonest. The confusion is brought about, I think, by a misunderstanding of the art of character. Hypocrisy is pretending to be something you are not, whereas Bernard Shaw pretended to be something that he really was. He really was the clownish, aggressive, loquacious G.B.S. as surely as he was the shy, careful Robert Smith. The principle of antinomy accounts for their co-existence, and neither was more real than the other. If anything, the public character was more real than the private if we define "the real" in terms of intensity. Here, however, I define "the real" as that which exists legitimately within the individual being; and certainly Robert Smith is as legitimate to the being of Shaw as, if less intense than, Ned Conolly, Sidney Trefusis, Owen Jack, Cashel Byron–Lydia Carew, or G.B.S.

Shaw called himself a "born actor," and to the actor within

14. In *Days with Bernard Shaw,* p. 262, Stephen Winsten reports Shaw as saying, "It is better to die a gentleman than a martyr."

him the many parts included in the general role of G.B.S. were quite natural. They provided a repertoire within the limits of which he almost always remained. He very well understood that to go outside this repertoire was to invite failure. He has recorded at least one attempt at a false impersonation: "I dramatized myself as George Vandaleur Lee, not very successfully, as the impersonation was false and foreign to my nature."[15] Shaw understood that it was an act of hypocrisy to play a role illegitimate to one's being; that is the source of the modern "phony." In going outside the limits of his own legitimate being, the phony invades and violates the character rights of others by creating the impression of falsity about the general character he is impersonating, which after all may be legitimate to someone else.

Bernard Shaw sometimes understood what I have been saying about the reality of his mask, but sometimes he seemed not to. Occasionally he would declare his public self to be a sham, a "mere" fiction, a deliberate calculation in his propaganda war against folly.[16] He would fight folly with folly. But that is not the whole truth. Eric Bentley explains it as well as anyone:

> True to Shavian formula the force that moved Shaw without his knowing whence or why was wiser than his conscious intention. If one can see this, one can see that even the creation of the "fantastic personality" was not merely

15. Henderson, p. 946.

16. In *Sixteen Self-Sketches,* p. 124, Shaw wrote the following about himself in the third person (originally written as a personal favor for Frank Harris' posthumous biography of Shaw): "Shaw is an incorrigible and continuous actor, using his skill as deliberately in his social life as in his professional work in the production of his own plays. He does not deny this. 'G.B.S.' he says 'is not a real person: he is a legend created by myself: a pose, a reputation. The real Shaw is not a bit like him.' Now this is exactly what all his acquaintances say of the Rodin bust, that it is not a bit like him. But Shaw maintains that it is the only portrait that tells the truth about him." Shaw must have enjoyed writing this passage, as it allowed him to play three or four different roles at once; but the reader is left with the inference that the supposedly fraudulent G.B.S. "is the only portrait that tells the truth about him."

the mistake of a bad strategist. Shaw's creation of "G.B.S." was not solely the deliberate, Machiavellian creation he tells us about. It too was created by the Life Force, by the World's Will. By all means it is a mask. But then it is part of the Shavian philosophy that life offers us not a choice between face and mask but only a choice between one mask and another. The "natural character" which he calls "impossible on the great London stage," the stammering blushing young Protestant from Dublin, this also was a "role," though a bad one. Silly and self-defeating as "G.B.S." can be, he too has his divine spark. "Every jest is an earnest in the womb of time"—even the jests of a foolish-looking mask.[17]

The distinction is thus between mask and mask, not between face and mask. Bentley's distinction is valuable in that it avoids the true and false connotations of face and mask. It is not the idea of the face that is objectionable so much as the idea that the mask is somehow less real than the face behind it.

Bentley feels that it is more accurate to speak of the alternation or juxtaposition of masks rather than of the mask overlaying the face. But a scene in *An Unsocial Socialist* suggests that the latter is more accurate. There is a scene showing Smilash going into the cottage and seconds later Trefusis coming out that particularly reminds me of the comic strip technique of "Superman." Clark Kent, "mild-mannered reporter," disappears into a closet and seconds later out pops Superman, blue cape and bulging biceps. But which is the disguise? We are told that Clark Kent is really Superman and that Smilash is really Trefusis; but is it not equally true that Superman is really Clark Kent and Trefusis really Smilash? Bentley's way out is to declare them both impersonations.

I have said that Smilash is an expression of Shaw's decision to play the economic fool to the madness of King Capitalism. Eric Bentley explains this perfectly in another context: "If modern life was as unreasonable as King Lear, Shaw would cast himself

17. Eric Bentley, *Bernard Shaw, 1856–1950*, p. 217.

as the Fool. Trace the word *mad* through his plays and you will find that many of the finest characters and the finest actions have it applied to them. . . . Bernard Shaw resorted to some very bizarre shifts. Living in this queer, disgusting age he found he had to give the impression that his highest quality—a sort of delicate spirituality, purity, or holiness—was fooling when what he meant was that his fooling was holy. The devil's advocate was almost a sort of saint. The clown was something of a super-man."[18]

18. *Ibid.*, pp. 210–11.

The Romance of the Real

The Brownings. Any amount is written about the romance of the Brownings, but though their story is among the romances of the world, I doubt whether they are read at all. Gossip there will always be about them, but with the Webbs there can be no gossip; they will be remembered by their work. As I have said, the prophet of the race will be the political economist. There is nothing like prosaic work. I had a grand time on the vestry worrying about drains, dust destructors, and instituting women's lavatories. The Webbs made a romance of reality, and when I want good literature I go to them and know I get the whole truth. When a person takes you aside and asks you what rent you pay and whether your boots pinch, you know that he is interested in you. The Webbs had that curiosity about life in a magnanimous spirit; they missed nothing and saw everything. Charlotte got to know them because she wanted to do something with her money. [emphasis added]

BERNARD SHAW
From Winsten, *Days with Bernard Shaw*

The chief objection to fictitious romance is that it is seldom so romantic as the truth.

BERNARD SHAW
Immaturity

In Search of Father

According to Jacques Barzun, "Shaw belonged to a generation of artists uncommonly cursed by alcoholism, disease, drugs, and degrading sensuality. Yeats, we know, thought that a special curse had descended on his generation of gifted men; Shaw's moral intention is to restore a belief in the fact that an artist can be sane."[1] In the "sick" atmosphere of nineteenth-century estheticism and the artist's alienation from bourgeois society, Bernard Shaw did everything possible to disconnect himself from the "pure art" movement. He saw in its narrow concern a rejection of at least half of the life legitimate to a human being, and in its rejection the cause of its "sickness." So he publicized himself as the very opposite of an esthete, thereby leading critics of a later age, an age considerably less controlled in art by the esthete, to misunderstand his art. Eric Bentley explains the cause of the misunderstanding:

When he himself writes in an encyclopedia: "Mr. Bernard Shaw . . . substituted the theatre for the platform . . . as his chief means of propaganda," Shaw is making his excuses. Having chosen art rather than propaganda as his profession, he tries to make up for it by making his art as propagandistic as possible, or rather—which is a different thing —by *saying* that his art is as propagandistic as possible. . . . Not that there is anything untrue in the statement that Shavian drama is didactic and public. But it is personal and expressive as well, a fact which Shaw has been at some pains to conceal. . . . *Shaw's drama expresses his nature much more than it champions particular doctrines.* It even mirrors Shaw's life rather closely in a series of self-portraits.[2] [italics added]

1. Jacques Barzun, *The Energies of Art*, p. 272.
2. Eric Bentley, *Bernard Shaw*, pp. 203–4.

But if Shaw's art is more "personal and expressive" than pub-lic and informative, why did he abandon the novel for the more public arrangement of the theatre? Among other reasons, could it be that the novels were *too* private? Without mentioning the novels, Bentley explains the perfect fitness of the theatre:

> It is the very peculiar mixture of the public and the private which the theatre affords that makes it so apt to his needs. A play is a public occasion like a political meeting; it is a celebration like a church service; it is a performance like a concert; and it is a work of art communicated by imper-sonations, by masks. The theatre is a magical world within a world, more satisfactory to Shaw's purpose and tempera-ment than any other. . . . He had . . . entered the theatre because it was a world apart. The paradox of Shaw's art is that he spends his energies in refusing to let the theatre *remain* a world apart. If his artist's nature made him a theatre critic instead of a statesman, his puritan conscience made him use his critical articles for attacks on the conven-tions of art, on the pure artist Shakespeare . . . and on defenses of reality. If his artist's nature drove him to "un-reality" of the theatre, his puritan conscience drove him to take "reality" with him.[3]

Perhaps, as Bentley implies, the craving for public participa-tion in his private story was a prime motivation for Shaw's substituting drama for novel. As far as Shaw's drama is personal and expressive, his theatre takes on the aspect of a confessional; but insofar as it is public and informative, his theatre takes on the character of a pulpit. In either case, pulpit or confessional, it serves an essentially religious function. One of the drawbacks of the novel is that it was too secular and too private for the religious purposes of Shaw. The novel lacks the sense of com-munion that the group participation of drama gives, and it lacks the persuasive magic of liturgical performance. Drama, fur-ther, gives much greater reality to such affective devices of the preacher as gesture, facial expression, and tone of voice.

3. *Ibid.*

Exactly what is the religious purpose of Bernard Shaw? I think that almost all of Shaw's work and life can be understood as an adventure in search of "God," the ground of Being, Authority, Motive, and Reality. It seems that the search for a father is not the exclusive property of that other "fatherlandless fellow," James Joyce.[4]

We have seen how the Shavian hero is always essentially parentless and nationless. Cashel Byron's mother is the only parent to survive Shaw's general devastation of parents, and even she is alienated from her son. Further, Mrs. Byron is the living example of the parental neglect symbolized by the almost total absence of parentage in these novels. Our young hero is always alone, independent, and homeless, either a lodger in someone else's house, or the reluctant owner of something unreal like Wiltstoken Castle or Sallust's House, Heritages of the Past and Palaces of Art that are foreign to his nature and in which he resides very uncomfortably. In short, the Shavian hero is a man without a father, without a fatherland, and without a Heavenly Father. There is no "home," no center of authority, for him to consult or appeal to. He is his own authority. If there is to be any authority in the world, it must proceed from out the being of the Superman.

The answer to the question of Shaw's "fatherlessness" is intriguing more critics all the time. What is the source of the Shavian orphan? Personal experience or public strategy? A particular childhood or simply the human condition? The most recent answer is to be found in B. C. Rosset's *Shaw of Dublin: The Formative Years,* and a fascinating answer it is.[5] Mr. Rosset's controversial thesis, which he admits is ultimately unprovable, is that George Bernard Shaw was named not after George Carr Shaw but after George Vandeleur Lee, the third party of the *ménage à trois* that lasted in the Shaw household from sometime shortly before Bernard's birth (1856) until Lee and Mrs. Shaw decamped separately to London in the 1870's,

4. Shaw calls himself a "fatherlandless fellow" in the preface to *Immaturity,* p. xxxv.

5. B. C. Rosset, *Shaw of Dublin: The Formative Years.*

leaving George Carr and George Bernard behind. That Shaw was the bastard son of George Vandeleur Lee was suspected, Rosset believes, by both George Carr (thus his insistence upon calling his son "Bob") and by G.B.S. (thus his hatred of the name "George"). Rosset, further, reveals Shaw's obsession with the theme of "the foundling" by counting up the number of times it appears in his plays, his letters, and his conversations, and the total is truly impressive. It is even a bit astounding if you haven't been prepared for it by meeting in Shaw's novels such fascinating foundlings as Robert Smith–Harriet Russell, Ned Conolly, Owen Jack, Cashel Byron–Lydia Carew, and Sidney Trefusis (not to mention a score of minor characters), as they are left on our doorstep.

Rosset has made his case overwhelmingly suggestive, but he does not make nearly the capital with the novels that he could have, as I have already shown. After making passing reference to Smith's anonymous father and Smilash's "Mebbe I warnt born at all," he goes into detail only with *Cashel Byron's Profession*.

In that novel, Mrs. Byron makes a rather odd statement in answer to a question concerning Cashel's relatives: " 'I am the only relative he ever had, poor fellow,' said [she], with a pensive smile. Then, seeing an expression of astonishment on the doc tor's face, she added quickly, 'They are all dead.' "[6] According to Rosset, "Attention to Shaw's phrasing will show that Mrs. Byron is actually saying that her son never had any relatives (other than herself) and amending it a moment later to say that the relatives he never had were dead. . . . Shaw struck precisely the note he desired in an artful suggestion of an unknown father."[7] Cashel knows nothing about his people or his mother's, for, as he confesses to Lydia, his mother "boxed my ears one day for asking who my father was, and I took good care not to ask her again."[8] When Lydia attempts a reconciliation between Cashel and his mother, Mrs. Byron at first rather contemptu ously dismisses Cashel's pretensions to the hand of Lydia: "*You*

6. *Cashel Byron's Profession*, p. 3.
7. Rosset, p. 141.
8. *Cashel Byron's Profession*, p. 137.

marry Miss Carew! . . . Do you know, you silly boy, that—"
Unfortunately Cashel interrupts her with, "I know all about
it . . . what she is; and what I am; and the rest of it" so that we
never discover what she and her son knew.[9] But after she sees
that her son is determined to marry Lydia despite the implication
that he is baseborn, she reverses her strategy and divulges the
secret that Cashel will shortly be the heir of considerable property in Dorsetshire upon the death of Old Bingley Byron, his
father's bachelor brother, thus contradicting her previous statement that all his relatives were dead. When Byron wonders
about his title in that people used to insinuate that his mother
was never married at all, Mrs. Byron theatrically expresses
great indignation and surprise that there could be any doubt.
Cashel seems convinced by this of his noble birth, and so the
novel ends with our trueborn Ivanhoe marrying Princess Lydia
in what, for Shaw, was an incredibly never-never-land ending.
Rosset believes that the ending was pure wish-fulfillment. While
I agree that psychic necessity rather than a willingness to conform to Victorian fiction patterns was responsible for this ending, I am not so sure that it was simply a symbolic playing out
of Shaw's desire for legitimacy.

As far as Rosset is concerned, Shaw now has a new daddy,
one that he didn't particularly care for. That may be so, but of
course the foundling theme can be accounted for in other ways.
It may be no more, and no less, than an expression of the homelessness of genius amidst the decay and death of the old Victorian
father-figures. Indeed, I am sure that is exactly what it is. But
that does not exclude the possibility that a literal bastardy may
be the source of some of Shaw's art. I am not presenting an
alternative so much (although those who dislike Rosset's thesis
may take it as an alternative) as an extension of the idea to other
levels. I am certain that more important to Shaw than the search
for a literal father was the search for a fatherland and a Heavenly
Father. If he had suspicions about his parentage, he used them
as materials for an artful expression of his lifelong quest for a
secular "home" and a religious justification. Karl Marx (via the

9. *Ibid.*, p. 211.

Fabian Society) promised the "home" of universal socialism, and the Life Force provided the religious justification, but not before Shaw placed under suspicion all other kinds of fatherland and Heavenly Father.

The novels help us a good deal in understanding the search by the Irish immigrant for a "fatherland," a society that would both tolerate him and enable him to feel at home within it. As Victorian England seems no more hospitable to genius than the Dublin he had just abandoned, he seeks whatever hospitality he can find in supranational societies. At first Smith is just plain lost, at home nowhere really, least of all Islington or Perspective; but Ned Conolly by virtue of his American inventiveness finds a home in the society of Intellect. Owen Jack manages to find some solace in the society of Art. Cashel Byron is quite comfortable in the society of Physical Action, although he rightly marries Intellect in the person of Lydia Carew before attempting Parliament. Finally, the Marxian society provides the only home that Sidney Trefusis cares to reside in, far preferring it to Sallust's House. As these societies have in common an international or supranational character, they really have as their premise the abolition of all fatherlands. The new "fatherland" of universal socialism depends upon the removal of the old nationalistic fatherlands. We are all fathers and sons of one another, Shaw always insisted.

Because of their criminal opinions, disreputable behavior, or shabby appearance, the Shavian heroes find themselves ambivalently ostracized by conventional society, the same society that occasionally lionizes them for their talents. Thus, although there is no progression in the essential homelessness of the Shavian hero—he is always outside the presumably genteel society of his birth—there is progression in the way these Outsiders meet ostracism by placing themselves in larger societies which find them acceptable.[10] From the society of Intellect to the society of

10. In the preface to *Immaturity,* p. xliv, Shaw writes: "When I had to come out of the realm of imagination into that of actuality I was still uncomfortable. I was outside society, outside politics, outside sport, outside the Church. If the term had been invented then I should have been called

Art to the society of Physical Action to the Marxian society is a progression from extreme detachment to extreme commitment. The novels tell the story of how a very social young man, rendered outlaw by his original morality, becomes an "unsocial" socialist. The novels describe a circle. The friendly and rather gallant young man attempts society, is rebuffed, shoots back up into the skies from which he had descended, until one day he is coaxed down from his lofty station by Karl Marx to tread once again the ground of social being, this time as a "socializer" bent upon teaching those who had rejected him a lesson in good manners. This is what Shaw meant by "socialism." The new "fatherland" of universal socialism would consist of a brotherhood of gentlemen.

Shaw eventually came to see that the founding of a universal fatherland was not enough, that a Heavenly Father was needed to sanction human deeds. Although the novels do not tell the whole story of Shaw's religious development, they do show us the kind of young man who would require religious purpose to set him in motion. *An Unsocial Socialist* records his temporary celebration of the secular religion offered by that communist saint, Karl Marx. Yet not even the Marxian gospel escapes the critical debunking of the young devotee. For the faithful there should be no God but Marx, but almost immediately Shaw began casting suspicion upon the divinity of Papa Marx. His debunking of the class war, for instance, must have been one of the first to come from within the movement. Understanding the fallibility of Marx, Shaw cast about until he came up with the Life Force, the religious impulse that gave considerably higher sanction than Marx to Shavian behavior. Marx helped him establish his theory of the new international fatherland, but the Life Force provided him with the Heavenly Father he needed to authorize Shavian evangelism. That story, though, is reserved for the plays.

The Complete Outsider. But the epithet would have been appropriate only within the limits of British barbarism. The moment music, painting, literature, or science came into question the positions were reversed: it was I who was the Insider. I had the intellectual habit. . . ."

The Real Romanced

One of the more important points about Shaw's novels is the hero's lack of religious motive. His motives are ethical and sane enough, but they possess no consciousness of religious meaning. He is ethical and sane for the sake of being ethical and sane, not because ethics and sanity are part of a religious comprehension. As Shaw himself put it, "I . . . needed only a clear comprehension of life in the light of an intelligible theory: in short, a religion. . . . It was the lack of this . . . that lamed me in those early days."[1]

Yet, as I have shown, the heroes of the novels are natural-born champions of a Faith—Smith argues for a faith he cannot name, Conolly argues for Rationalism and Realism, Jack argues for Art, Byron argues for Active Good, and Trefusis argues for Socialism. The novels, in short, reveal Shaw's search for "an intelligible theory" of life by way of Rationalism, Realism, Aestheticism, Activism, and Socialism. But while these secular creeds provided him with motive power and reasons for living the good life, they did not provide him with the divine sanction he naturally craved. That is why the Shavian hero always seems so much like a chivalric figure off on a quest. The adventures of the hero in search of God involve him in a kind of romance, which, following Shaw's lead, I choose to call the "Romance of the Real."[2]

Robert Louis Stevenson seems to have understood the under-

1. *Immaturity,* p. xliv.
2. Shaw had a habit of projecting himself into the beings of others. He entitled a book *The Quintessence of Ibsenism* that he might more accurately have called *The Quintessence of Shaw.* Just so, in the epigraph to this section, he described the life of the Webbs in a way that would have more accurately fit himself—"The Webbs made a romance of reality." I take this to refer to his own ability to find religious truth in the midst of human detail, to convert a prosaic vestry meeting into a chivalric episode, for instance.

lying chivalry of Shaw's novels better than most. After reading
Cashel Byron's Profession he wrote to William Archer about the
young Shaw: "Let him beware of his damned century: his gifts
of insane chivalry and animated narration are just those that
might be slain and thrown out like an untimely birth by the
Daemon of the Epoch. . . . if he only knew how I had enjoyed
the chivalry!"[3] A bit later Stevenson wrote again to Archer:
"It is all mad, mad and deliriously delightful; the author has a
taste in chivalry like Walter Scott's or Dumas's, and then he
daubs in little bits of socialism; he soars away on the wings of the
romantic griffin—even the griffin, as he cleaves air, shouting with
laughter at the nature of the quest—and I believe in his heart he
thinks he is labouring in a quarry of solid granite realism. . . ."[4]
Stevenson was sharper than most in appreciating the discrepancy
between the seemingly realistic intent of Shaw's novels and the
romantic results, but he did not quite understand that, unlike
the case of Scott and Dumas, Shaw's romance was *in* the realism.

One of the chief characteristics of romance, in theory, is the
central role of Woman. Although the chivalric figure ultimately
serves God, he serves God principally by serving Woman, for
it is in her service that he is called upon to exercise all of those
virtues which mark him as a Godly man. Woman, further,
symbolizes all those qualities of beauty and perfection that are
attributes of Deity, and fulfills other sacred functions such as
the bestowing of "grace" and "beatitude." Most importantly,
it is through her constant inspiration that the hero is encouraged
to persevere in his quest for the ideal life.

The pattern of chivalry appears often in Shaw's novels, and
is perhaps best illustrated by *Immaturity*. From the very first,
Smith is identified as a chivalric figure, first by the Dürer drawing of a knight that he carries around with him, and second by
his reaction to the presence of Woman. No sooner does he encounter Harriet Russell than Smith conceives a romance. However homeless he may feel otherwise, the Shavian hero always
finds hospitality in the romance of Woman and can abide even

3. *Cashel Byron's Profession*, p. xix.
4. R. L. Stevenson, *Letters of Robert Louis Stevenson*, pp. 48–50.

in the heart of Victorian darkness if only it be illuminated by the smile of a likely female. Obviously Smith's response to Woman is conditioned by his need for encouragement. "Smith began to crave for a female friend who would encourage him to persevere in the struggle for truth and human perfection, during those moments when its exhilaration gave place to despair."[5]

Smith conducts three different romances during the course of the novel—with Isabella, with Harriet, and with the *prima ballerina* at "a very wicked place" called the Alhambra. Harriet at first failing to give him the encouragement he desires, Smith increasingly frequents the Alhambra to adore the young lady who is the only inspired performer in an otherwise very uninspired ballet entitled "The Golden Harvest." His adoration of the dancer has a wonderful effect on him: "The dancer, instead of occupying his imagination to the exclusion of everything else, became a centre of mental activity, and caused one of those ruptures of intellectual routine which . . . are valuable as occasions of fresh departures in thought."[6] He becomes learned in the history of ballet and the traditions of the opera, and begins "to entertain notions of becoming a composer."[7] Reminiscent of Shaw's later affair with Ellen Terry, Smith's worship of his beloved dancer thrives on esthetic distance. He never meets her. Because of its obviously artificial quality, Smith is alternately exhilarated and disgusted by his purely imaginary love affair.

The romance comes to an end when Smith is fed a sordid tale about the real life of the dancer that bitterly disillusions him. "Smith believed it all because it made him feel completely disillusioned. Men easily mistake the shock of disillusion for the impact of brute truth. As a matter of fact the whole tale . . . was a shameless fiction."[8] Had Smith known the real story of the dancer, that of a struggling young artist trying to uphold the tradition of the grand school of Italian dancing, perhaps "Smith would have fallen in love with her more hopelessly than ever." The

5. *Immaturity*, p. 83.
6. *Ibid.*, pp. 78–79.
7. *Ibid.*, p. 78.
8. *Ibid.*, p. 125.

Shavian moral is that "the chief objection to fictitious romance is that it is seldom so romantic as the truth." The experience was probably for the better, Shaw advises, as it made Smith "realize that the dancer was a human being, and his dreams about her something that could never be realized even if he rescued her every night from a runaway hansom. . . ."[9]

Shortly after Smith's disillusionment with the dancer, the Alhambra becomes a volcano of flames and burns to the ground.[10] With perfect timing, however, the spirit of romance rises phoenix-like out of the ashes of the Alhambra in the person of Isabella Woodward, an Irish colleen. Though the name Isabella continues the Spanish connotation of the name Alhambra, Smith's romance with Isabella is of a very different sort, as the impossible romance of the ideal dancer is replaced by the very possible romance of the very real Isabella. Spanish romance by way of earthy Ireland is a very different thing from Spanish romance pure in spirit. The romance of Isabella is the romance of a human being, complete with sexual contact (a few kisses, in Smith's case). Its nexus is flirtation because it is essentially a holiday affair, not to be taken seriously, and does not itself take seriously anything so serious as marriage. Marriage is the viola-tion of the courtly sense, which sees in marriage the death of love. That is why marriage seems to have nothing to do with Smith, and why he would never have dreamed of inventing it. The true chevalier cannot in his chivalric soul bear to deny any attractive female his romantic patronage. The more devoted he is to his Lady, the more devoted he is to all ladies.

Smith is momentarily entertained by the romance of Isabella, but we must note that he concludes it with relief. I think it further significant that Shaw ends the novel by having Smith return to Harriet. Smith's pilgrimage to Harriet for the verdict of his immaturity signifies Shaw's own psychic preference for realism in human affairs. When Harriet returns to Islington after her trip to Richmond, Smith sees her on the stairs and compares

9. *Ibid.*, p. 126.
10. A catastrophe that recalls the complete demolition of the Islington lodging house. Smith leaves nothing behind!

her with the Alhambra dancer: "Her appearance in the morning sunlight made him feel as though he had just stepped from that vile-smelling midnight vision of gilt sheaves, painted skies, and electric radiance, into a real harvest field, full of fresh air, noisy birds, and sunshine."[11] Smith is already developing a Shavian preference for reality over "romantic" illusion, but only because reality is more "romantic."

Of the three romances of Robert Smith—the romance of Ideal Beauty, the romance of Real Beauty, and the romance of the Real—his first and his last is the romance of the Real.[12] Romantically speaking, the book begins and ends with Harriet. The romance of Ideal Beauty, exhilarating while it lasts, ends in disgust and disillusionment; the romance of Real Beauty ends in flirtation; the only romance that endures is the romance of the Real. Smith's adoration of Ideal Beauty is a serious enough thing, as becomes a devout Shelleyan, but by its impossibilist nature it can only end in disgust and disillusionment. That is the inevitable conclusion to such adoration unless one has the courage to meet the Alhambra dancer and convert her romance into a romance of the Real. As Shaw says, that would have been *more* romantic. Smith's flirtation with Real Beauty is strictly a holiday thing, as it partakes of the ephemeral excitements of lovemaking. There is reality here, but it is the reality of playtime, of the child in man. It is all right for a while, but as it is by nature impulsive and inconstant, it is not to be taken as anything more than recreation. Ultimately Smith comes to prefer the romance of the Real as more romantic than the other two. The romance of the Real provides both the intellectual stimulation and the emotional encouragement provided separately by the other two, and provides it without the disillusionment of the one and the tedious

11. *Immaturity,* p. 80.

12. These three types of romance seem to correspond to the three types of people Shaw classified in *The Quintessence of Ibsenism.* The romance of Ideal Beauty is the romance for Idealists, the romance of Real Beauty the romance for Philistines, and the romance of the Real the romance for Realists. That Shaw could indulge in all three types of romances is perhaps recognition of the fact that he contained within himself all three types of people.

hedonism of the other. But at first Smith lacks an appreciation of the Real. The Real naturally has imperfections, and the adorer of Ideal Beauty finds them insurmountable, for a time, to the continuation of his romance. Later, just as Harriet reconsiders her judgment of Smith, Smith too raises his estimation of Harriet. Harriet's sensible remark about marriage—"What else is one to do if one is to have a decent home?"—is the sort of realistic comment about human affairs that Shaw admired for its frank acceptance of life, and its implied willingness to make a romance out of that reality. At the same time, the remark indicates a clearsightedness that will not allow any delusions harmful to either mind or body.

Despite his preference for the Real, Shaw throughout his lifetime managed to carry on all three kinds of romance. The early adolescent part of his life was dominated by the Shelleyan intellectual's romance of Ideal Beauty, the young manhood part by the philanderer's romance of Real Beauty, and the middle-aged part by the domesticated husband's romance of the Real. The Ellen Terry romance, conducted by letter, is much like the romance of Ideal Beauty, although Ellen Terry herself had some of the qualities of Harriet. Shaw knew this and tried to convert that romance into a romance of the Real, but only half-heartedly, as they both seemed to rather enjoy the remoteness of their romance. He watched her on the stage, and she peeked at him through the curtains. As the Ellen Terry romance appealed to the most youthful part of Shaw, he must have been reluctant to give it up. His later philandering with "Stella" Campbell is very similar to Smith's romance with Isabella, even to the point of fleshly contact out of wedlock, and his affair with Charlotte Payne-Townshend is similar to Smith's romance with Harriet, although in Charlotte's case Shaw took Harriet's advice ("What else is one to do if one is to have a decent home?") and married her. While Shaw fruitlessly worshipped Miss Terry from afar, and merely philandered with Stella, he married the Real and lived with her. That is, while Shaw's diverse personality seemed to require all three kinds of romance, his preference and most lasting affection was for the Real.

Jacques Barzun comes closest to explaining what I mean by "the romance of the real":

> Perhaps an iconoclast is always a man who destroys cheap images rather than ancient ones. At any rate, it is one of the oldest of all Western ideas—the idea of Christianity— which is in Shaw the central and lasting one. Shaw is a fundamentalist Christian; only, he insists that the traditional words be compelled to carry an active meaning. For him Sin, Revelation, the Communion of Saints, the Life Everlasting, the necessity of Gospel Love, are truths of experience. But they must be kept empirically true by continual re-embodiment, resisting time's burial of live meaning under the crust of habit. Charity, for example, can no longer mean giving coins to beggars; it must mean making war on poverty. Finding the means to the end is the task of the righteous, God's work.[13]

That is, Shaw found the reality of Christian experience considerably more romantic than the fictions of formalized religion, just as he found the reality of political and economic engagement more romantic than the fictions of Walter Scott, or the reality of marriage to Charlotte more romantic than the philandering with Stella. Religion for him was something that happens in the street, not a ritual calisthenic to be exercised indoors on a Sunday morning; and the happening in the street was much more romantic, i.e., inspiring in its heroism, than however many exercises in organized religion's spiritual gymnasiums. (At first Robert Smith heartily enjoys his visions of "destroyed churches and confuted priests," but as Shaw matured he came to feel that the "calisthenics" perhaps did some good after all, provided that they were looked upon as *preparations* for religious action rather than as the whole of religion.)

Perhaps it was in the municipal realities of Fabian socialism that Shaw found his greatest romance. For Shaw, socialism was a political, social, and economic system for the regeneration of

13. *The Energies of Art,* pp. 270–71.

society, to be sure, but it also was a metaphor for something else. It was unlike Shaw to give his allegiance to something so ephemeral as a social system unless that system somehow gave expression to something more deeply permanent in human affairs. Socialism was a figure of speech that referred to the only possible public response a Christian Gentleman of the nineteenth century could make to the Industrial Capitalism that had made a mockery of traditional charity, not to mention all the other values of the traditional gentleman and the traditional Christian. When private charity availed not, it was necessary to organize it as part of the system. Eric Bentley explains this well:

> The socialism of Carlyle, Ruskin, Shaw, of what I have called the British "aristocratic" line, is not scientific; it is ethical. Their belief in humanity is not faith in the common man but in the gentleman. For the gentleman is a synthesis of the democrat and the aristocrat, the follower and the leader. He is a living symbol of the fact that aristocracy is not something to be superseded but to be included in democracy, that the nobleman, if he has ceased to be a robber baron, is welcome in the new age, that we, as much as Louis XIV or George III, need men of light and leading. Moreover the gentlemanly ideal is the golden mean between two rival types—the priest and the soldier, the Pope and the Emperor or, in more recent language, the yogi and the commissar. That is why the British genius, which is for temperance, did not wait for Shaw before it formulated this ideal. Not only Carlyle and Ruskin, but such contrasted doctrinaires as Burke, Newman, and T. H. Huxley were spokesmen for it.[14]

In an off-the-cuff speech addressed to the National Liberal Club in 1913 Shaw said:

> What is the ideal of the gentleman? The gentleman makes a certain claim on his country to begin with. He makes a

14. *Bernard Shaw*, pp. 34–35.

claim for a handsome and dignified existence and subsistence; and he makes that as a primary thing not to be depended on his work in any way; not to be doled out
according to the things he has done or according to the
talents that he has displayed. He says, in effect: "I want to
be a cultured human being; I want to live in the fullest
sense; I require a generous subsistence for that; and I expect
my country to organize itself in such a way as to secure me
that." Also the real gentleman says—and here is where the
real gentleman parts company with the sham gentleman, of
whom we have so many: "In return for that I am willing to
give my country the best service of which I am capable;
absolutely the best. My ideal shall be also that, no matter
how much my country has given me, I hope and I shall
strive to give to my country in return more than it has given
to me; so that when I die my country shall be the richer for
my life. . . ." The real constructive scheme you want is the
practical inculcation into everybody that what the country
needs, and should seek through its social education, its
social sense, and religious feeling, is to create gentlemen;
and, when you create them, all other things shall be added
unto you.[15]

There is the Superman. Not much more than the gentleman of
the Renaissance humanists' conception, itself a derivative of the
earlier Chivalric ideal, and both products of the synthesis between the best in Christian and pagan thought. Shaw's call for
the Superman was simply an attempt to restore a sense of values
in an age in which worth was leveled by the democratic impulse,
and a sense of social cohesion in an age in which life was frag-
mented by the capitalistic impulse.

Of course Shaw said a lot of harsh things about the English
"gentleman," but all this was like his being anti-romantic,
anti-Christian, or anti-art; he did that precisely because he
was a "shining knight," a "Christian," an "artist," and a "gentleman." This was his way of distinguishing the false from the

15. *Ibid.*, pp. 35–36.

real, the dead from the living. If Yahoos are going to call themselves "men," then true men have no choice but to call themselves "Supermen." If irreligious people are going to call themselves "religious," then truly religious men have no choice but to call themselves "irreligious." If esthetes are going to call themselves "artists," then true artists must call themselves "propagandists." If crooks are going to call themselves "decent, respectable, law-abiding citizens," then true citizens must call themselves "enemies of the people."

And that is the story of Shaw's novels. They show us the romance of a young Christian gentleman, possessed of the gift of irony, gradually distinguishing himself from his Victorian surroundings, discovering the cause of his outlawry, and devising the strategy of the Ironist. The Superman—the Christian Gentleman—pretends to be the Satan that everyone thought he was, so that intelligent men could recognize and laugh at the discrepancy between the true man and the reputed devil.

The novels, thus, deal with the special problems of young, unproved genius in adapting to a hostile environment, an adaptation that involves him in a birth sequence as he passes into the womb of art before emerging a fully effective adult. *Immaturity* records the impregnation of the Shavian idea—Robert Smith being appropriately fetal in his undefined shapelessness (note the anonymity of the name "Smith"); the next three novels recapitulate the shaping of genius through the stages of intellectual development, emotional development, and the synthesis of mind and body, concluding with the birth of a relatively complete human being recorded in the final novel. The appendix to *An Unsocial Socialist* can be read as the cutting of the cord. Fittingly coming at the end of Shaw's incubation period in the British museum, the last novel marks the opening of his public career. Shaw had worked out in private art the basic design of his public future, fulfilling his own dictum that "No person is real until he has been transmuted into a work of art."

Selected Bibliography

Works by Shaw

An Unfinished Novel, ed. Stanley Weintraub. New York: Dodd, Mead, 1958.

Collected Letters 1874–1897, ed. Dan H. Laurence. New York: Dodd, Mead, 1965.

Complete Plays with Prefaces. 6 vols. New York: Dodd, Mead, 1963.

Ellen Terry and Bernard Shaw: A Correspondence, ed. Christopher St. John. New York: Theater Arts Books, 1932.

Fabian Essays in Socialism, ed. Shaw. New York: Doubleday & Co., Inc., 1963.

Florence Farr, Bernard Shaw, W. B. Yeats, Letters, ed. Clifford Bax. London: Home & Van Thal Ltd., 1946.

The Matter with Ireland, ed. Dan H. Laurence. New York: Hill and Wang, 1962.

"Mr. Bernard Shaw's Works of Fiction Reviewed by Himself," *Novel Review,* No. 33 (February, 1892), pp. 236–243.

My Dear Dorothea, ed. Stephen Winsten. New York: Vanguard Press, 1963.

Platform and Pulpit, ed. Dan H. Laurence. New York: Hill and Wang, 1961.

Standard Edition of the Works of Bernard Shaw. London: Constable & Co., Ltd., 1931–32.

Secondary Sources

Abbott, Anthony S. *Shaw and Christianity.* New York: The Seabury Press, 1965.

Barzun, Jacques. *The Energies of Art.* New York: Vintage Books, 1962.

Bentley, Eric. *Bernard Shaw, 1856–1950,* rev. ed. New York: New Directions Paperback, 1957.

Bissell, Claude T. "The Novels of Bernard Shaw," *The University of Toronto Quarterly,* XVII (1947–48), 50–51.

Borges, Jorge Luis. *Other Inquisitions, 1937–1952.* New York: Washington Square Press, 1960.

Chappelow, Allan, ed. *Shaw the Villager and Human Being.* New York: The Macmillan Co., 1962.

Chesterton, G. K. *George Bernard Shaw*. New York: Hill and Wang, 1958.

Collis, John S. *Shaw*. New York: Alfred A. Knopf, Inc., 1924.

Dietrich, R. F. "Shaw and the Passionate Mind," *The Shaw Review,* IV (May, 1961), 2–11.

Henderson, Archibald. *George Bernard Shaw: Man of the Century*. New York: Appleton-Century-Crofts, Inc., 1956.

Henderson, Archibald. "Where Shaw Stands Today," *Bulletin of the Shaw Society of America,* I (Autumn, 1951), 1–6.

Hogan, Robert. "The Novels of Bernard Shaw," *English Literature in Transition 1880–1920,* VIII (1965), 63–114.

Huneker, James. "Bernard Shaw and Women," *Harper's Bazaar,* XXXIX (June, 1905), 535–38.

Irvine, William. *The Universe of G.B.S.* New York: McGraw-Hill, 1949.

Karl, Frederick R. *The Contemporary English Novel*. New York: Farrar, Straus, and Cudahy, 1962.

Morgan, Charles. *The House of Macmillan, 1843–1943*. London: Macmillan, 1943.

Nethercot, Arthur H. *Men and Supermen: The Shavian Portrait Gallery*. Cambridge: Harvard University Press, 1954.

O'Donnell, Norbert F. "The Conflict of Wills in Shaw's Tragicomedy," *Modern Drama,* IV (February, 1962), 413–25.

Ohmann, Richard M. *Shaw: The Style and the Man*. Middletown, Conn.: Wesleyan University Press, 1962.

Pearson, Hesketh. *George Bernard Shaw: His Life and Personality*. New York: Atheneum, 1963.

Rattray, R. F. *Bernard Shaw: A Chronicle*. New York: Roy Publishers, 1951.

Rao, E. Nageswara. *Shaw the Novelist: A Critical Study of Shaw's Narrative Fiction*. Masulipatam: Triveni Publishers, 1959.

Rodenbeck, John von Behren. "Alliance and Misalliance: A Critical Study of Bernard Shaw's Novels." Dissertation. University of Virginia, 1964.

Rosset, B. C. *Shaw of Dublin: The Formative Years*. University Park: Pennsylvania State University Press, 1964.

Saroyan, William. *Here Comes–There Goes–You Know Who*. New York: Pocket Books, Inc., 1963.

Smith, Warren S. "The Bishop, the Dancer, and Bernard Shaw," *The Shaw Review,* III (January, 1960), 2–10.

Stanbrook, the Benedictines of. *In a Great Tradition*. London: Murray, 1956.

Stevenson, R. L. *Letters of Robert Louis Stevenson*, III, rev. ed., ed. Sidney Colvin. New York: Charles Scribners Sons, 1896.

Weintraub, Stanley. "Bernard Shaw: Novelist." Dissertation. University Park: Pennsylvania State University, 1956.

Weintraub, Stanley. "The Embryo Playwright in Bernard Shaw's Early Novels," *University of Texas Studies in Literature and Language,* I (1959), 327–55.

Winsten, Stephen. *Days with Bernard Shaw.* New York: Vanguard Press, Inc., 1949.

Woodbridge, Homer. *George Bernard Shaw: Creative Artist.* Carbondale: Southern Illinois University Press, 1963.